THE WORLD CUP CHRONICLES
31 Days That Rocked Brazil

JORGE KNIJNIK

Jorge Knijnik was born in Porto Alegre, capital city of Rio Grande do Sul, Brazil's southernmost state. It was on the stands of the Grêmio Football Porto Alegrense Estádio Olímpico and most of all, on the cemented stands of the Pacaembu Stadium in São Paulo city's heart, that he started his career as a football fan.

After spending numerous afternoons standing side by side with his dad under heavy rain to watch Pelé alive on the Pacaembu pitch, Jorge began to intuitively understand the unique cultural power that football has to strengthen social relationships. During his adolescence and as a young man, he followed his beloved São Paulo FC across Brazil and South America during the most successful period of the club's history, winning two Copa Libertadores da America titles.

In 2009, Jorge migrated to Australia with his young family and continued to actively follow football on the stands, supporting the Western Sydney Wanderers FC. He is also a volunteer coach in grassroots football clubs and an activist for gender and ethnic inclusion in the game.

Jorge currently works as an Associate Professor in the School of Education and the Institute for Culture & Society at Western Sydney University in Australia. His overarching research interests focus on topics of mega sports events and social justice, gender, multiculturalism, sport education, critical football studies and social inclusion.

Most of his written works can be found at https://uws.academia.edu/JorgeKnijnik and you can follow his football adventures @JorgeKni

THE WORLD CUP CHRONICLES

CHRONICLES

31 Days that Rocked Brazil

Jorge Knijnik

FAIRPLAY
PUBLISHING

FAIRPLAY
PUBLISHING

First published in 2018 by Fair Play Publishing
PO Box 4101, Balgowlah Heights NSW 2093 Australia
www.fairplaypublishing.com.au
sales@fairplaypublishing.com.au

ISBN: 978-0-6481333-1-5
ISBN: 978-0-6481333-3-9 (ePUB)

Design and typesetting by Retta Laraway, Looksee Design.

Front cover: by Marcia Zoet: *A girl shows super ball control in a Rio favela*

Back cover: by Ana Carolina Fernandes *World Cup = extermination, and Progress is not order*

Other photographs by Ana Carolina Fernandes, Lulu di Mello, Luciana Whitaker.

NATIONAL
LIBRARY
OF AUSTRALIA

A catalogue record for this
book is available from the
National Library of Australia

Disclaimer

For Caloca and Babi,
beloved parents

CONTENTS

Part 1: Imagining the World Cup

Part 2: Living the World Cup

Part 3: The after match: what kind of legacy?

PREFACE

By Roger Kittleson

In purely sporting terms the one inescapable, irreparable fact that emerged from the 2014 World Cup in Brazil can be summed up in two digits: 7 and 1. Seven to one, of course, was the defeat imposed by an excellent German team on a hapless home side. The game was even more lopsided than that ridiculous score line suggests, worse even than pessimistic Brazil supporters feared. (Brazil had looked shaky in previous games, so I told my wife that I hoped we would not see a 3-0 loss; the Germans scored five unanswered goals in the opening half-hour.) It was so bad, in fact, that it sparked a grim optimism in some quarters: Such a shameful result at home would surely force officials to clean up the organizational "anarchy" that had characterised the national sport for decades.

It was not only this one gruesome match, however, that inspired a mixture of feelings among Brazilians. Both the preparations for the 2014 World Cup, only the second held in the country, and the tournament itself fuelled powerful emotions from joy to utter despair. Nationalistic pride greeted the 2007 announcement that Brazil had been chosen to host the Cup. Then-president Luis Inácio Lula da Silva declared that the megaevent would cement Brazil as "first-class" country, and few voiced any disagreement. In the lead-up to 2014, though, the general mood was mixed—if, indeed, anything like a general mood remained.

The costs of mounting the tournament proved greater than anyone had predicted, in social as well as economic terms. Taxpayers found themselves on the hook for grandiose plans concocted by high-handed politicians and FIFA administrators, just as the country's economy began a serious slowdown. Against that background, a small movement pressing for free bus fares in São Paulo blossomed into wide scale protest. The initial cause was soon almost forgotten, as Brazilians took the opportunity to air a wide range of complaints.

An amazingly wide range of citizens took to the streets in cities across the country, seeking justice for those mistreated by the police, an end to political corruption, and other major reforms.

Although the largest protests occurred during the 2013 Confederations Cup – a sort of dress rehearsal held before each World Cup – the great competition of 2014 became, in Jorge Knijnik's apt phrase, "31 days that shook the world." The traumatic defeat of the *Seleção* was, in the end, just one of the challenges that emerged during the World Cup, and perhaps not even one of the most serious of them. As has always been the case, soccer here served as a space in which Brazilians could talk about the most grave problems facing their nation. Unlike most earlier periods, though, their conversations rarely had the lightness of sports chats; in 2014 Brazil the World Cup felt serious, and discussions about the *Seleção* seemed inseparable from considerations of the political and economic strains that were polarizing the country, although the exact nature of the sides in conflict was anything but clear. At the same time, this World Cup came not only as the Brazilian state but also the world governing body of soccer, FIFA, came under heightened scrutiny.

Few were as well positioned as Jorge to put these grand processes into context even as they were unfolding. He had already produced brilliant studies of Brazilian soccer and the development of the national style; his work has always dug into the power dynamics at work in this history, even as his love of "the beautiful game" shines through. As a Brazilian who has made his career outside the country, moreover, he brings a wonderful "insider-outsider" perspective to his observations of the 2014 World Cup. He picks up on details that non-Brazilians might not even notice and applies his deep knowledge of the history of Brazil and its futebol to explain their broad significance. More often, though, he takes us to the most dramatic events and personalities – the demonstrations in 2013 and their more muted sequels during the 2014 tournament, the captivating play of stars past and present, alongside the distasteful behaviour of politicians and sports administrators. Here, he forces us to confront the momentous questions that the World Cup posed, and not only for Brazilians: What does soccer mean in an ever-more tightly networked world? How do sports and the incredible business that they have become shape our understanding of ourselves as citizens of our cities, our nations, our world? How do Brazilians–or anyone–try to take control over their lives, win rights they are due as citizens, and combat corruption and government abuses in the twenty-first century?

In these chronicles, Jorge Knijnik leads us to consider such grand issues. Along the way, though, he tells the fascinating stories of the coaches and players who have made Brazilian soccer such an iconic phenomenon, as well as the stadiums in which they have performed (and those in which very few people will ever perform again) and the powerful figures who oversaw the decline of "the nation of football" so sadly apparent in the 7-1 loss. Most of all, Jorge focuses on common people of his home country, introducing us to women and men who battle great odds to make Brazil serve its population more justly. The vivid commitment they show, with a vibrant mixture of optimism and practicality, runs through these pages, echoing the author's own passionate take on the nation of his birth and, with any luck, inspiring similar feelings in all those who read this remarkable book.

Roger Kittleson

West Harford, Connecticut

August 2017

Roger Kittleson is Professor of History at Williams College.

INTRODUCTION

South Africa (2010); Brazil (2014) ... and Russia (2018): the BRICS way of delivering a FIFA World Cup

It was not a coincidence that the three FIFA World Cups of this decade were hosted or will be hosted by one of the so-called BRICS countries (Brazil, Russia, India, China and South Africa).

The BRICS have not only hosted this decade's FIFA World Cups but they have also hosted several Olympic-alike events in the past 12 years (2007 Rio Pan-American Games; 2008 Beijing and 2016 Rio Olympic Games; 2010 Delhi Commonwealth Games; 2014 Sochi Winter Olympic Games).

Mega sport events such as the world's marquee football tournament are clearly key elements of the BRICS' international diplomatic strategy. It looks like these countries want to assert themselves not only in the economic area, but in terms of their global profile.

It is not also accidental that the sports events in these countries, particularly the World Cups, have so many similarities. On the one hand, the FIFA tournaments always bring high-levels of public engagement, short-term thrill and a long-term questionable legacy to the host countries. On the other hand, they leave a track of frauds, disrupted communities and ambiguous political pacts.

The parallels between the 'BRICS World Cups' start in their successful but controversial bids. These bids had mixed in the same pot political pay-backs, an incredible amount of bribes and obscure financial deals. These FIFA methods had long been denounced by a few journalists such as British investigative journalist Andrew Jennings. However, they attracted much more international public attention after the FBI intervened and arrested several high-level FIFA officers in the 2015 Zurich detentions. Their exposure in the US courts continues to reveal the extent of the corruption networks inside the international football community.

South Africa, Brazil and Russia are exemplary cases of what a FIFA tournament can entail. Ricardo Teixeira, former president of the Brazilian Football Federation (CBF) and chair of the 2014 World Cup Local Organising Committee was forced to step down from his positions two years prior to the tournament that he brought to Brazil. Jose Maria Marin, who replaced Teixeira as the Brazilian chief of the 2014 World Cup local organising committee, is in custody in the US since the Zurich arrests and consequently, has been banned from his roles at FIFA. Marin is expected to spend the rest of his life in a US Federal jail.

What is next now? Will the Brazilian judicial authorities ever investigate whether Marin's crimes had any ramifications over the country's institutions? Will the powerful Rede Globo ever be investigated? After all, the largest Brazilian broadcaster was in the centre of most of the deals over football competitions broadcasting rights for so many years with Marin, and his partners.

On the other hand, it took FIFA more than two years until the end of 2017 to suspend Marco Polo Del Nero, Marin's political partner and deputy for many years, from his position as the president of the Brazilian Football Federation. This suspension only happened after strong evidence against him surfaced in the US FIFA trials. Prior to that, he lost his position at FIFA's executive committee but still reigned for more than two years in the powerful national federation, without any questioning from the international body. As I write this book, the football world awaits what will be next for Del Nero.

In Russia, Vitaly Mutko, former deputy minister for sport and chief of the 2018 World Cup local organising committee, finally stepped down from his football positions at the end of 2017. Despite his alleged roles in the Russian doping scandals, FIFA supported him till the end, as FIFA's president stood by his side in front of the international press when Mutko stepped down, denying all allegations against him.

The downfalls in the BRICS World Cup Local Organising Committees did not surprise people who closely follow FIFA's internal political games. Perhaps the surprise was that Danny Jordaan, the chair of the South Africa Local Organising Committee, remained in his position to the end of the competition, despite several bribery allegations against him.

The correspondences between the BRICS World Cups do not stop in the political manoeuvres of the top-hats neither in the bribes scandals. A World Cup involves much more than the dubious actions of local and international football leaders.

The FIFA tournament brings an incredible amount of disruption to the local communities where it is held. The host countries' plans are always to build the 'much needed' sporting and touristic infrastructure in the hosting cities, while promoting their positive image across the world and attracting further tourism beyond the football period.

Nevertheless, FIFA's demands for state-of-the-art stadiums for the World Cup regularly find vulnerable communities in the way of construction. Violent relocations of these communities have been the BRICS' standard procedure.

Moreover, the amount of stadiums that become white elephants after the World Cup is well-known by the public. In South Africa, a few white elephants that have not been used since the 2010 event are the stadium Mbombela Stadium in Mpumalanga Province, the Cape Town Stadium, and the Nelson Mandela stadium in Port Elizabeth. To add an extra hurdle for the local communities, the municipalities must maintain these stadiums with an elevated cost.

The situation is identical in Brazil with FIFA-standard stadiums begging for help just a few months after the end of the tournament. The Arena Amazonia in Manaus and Arena Pantanal in Cuiabá are examples of white elephants specifically built for the World Cup in regions where there is no sufficient professional football activity to justify the existence of big stadiums. Even the Mané Garrincha stadium, built in Brasilia (Brazil's federal capital) is another white elephant that still burdens the local community with its high operational costs.

Yet, a World Cup is not only about problems. There is plenty of enjoyment and remarkable real-life stories happening with people's daily lives during the tournaments. These accounts are also similar throughout the host cities and countries. These are the stories that this book tells. It conveys tales about the traditional cultures that resisted FIFA's demands. It talks about school teachers who took advantage of their students' interest in the World Cup to plan and deliver authentic learning lessons to their classrooms. It unveils historic rivalries between the countries in the subcontinent.

The accounts are endless and show how ordinary people can benefit from the 'invasion' of their country by the World Cup circus. These stories happened during the 2014 Brazil World Cup. Still, with some local cultural adjustments, they describe what could have happened in South Africa or may well happen in Russia.

The World Cup chronicles are not only made up by the top people's deceit and egoistic behaviour. They were (and they will be) mainly performed by the ordinary people that lived and endured all the disturbances brought by the major event. Yet, most of them survived and even found the strength to cheer on their national teams.

The stories in this book were written by a Brazilian with deep knowledge of Brazilian culture and history. They talk about Brazil and Brazilians before, during and after the World Cup. But they could have also been written by a South African or by a Russian with great familiarity of their culture and people.

After all, in terms of a BRICS World Cup, South Africa = Brazil = Russia. By narrating Brazil's chronicles, the book reminds us how amazing the resemblances between the events in these different countries are.

Using a daily-life perspective, this book opens the door for future similar explorations of the World Cup's impacts in the everyday lives of citizens. As important as the major economic and social effects of sport mega-events are, they only count when people see and feel their own existence rocked by a World Cup.

Jorge Knijnik

Sydney, Australia

June 2018

Note: The acronym BRIC was coined in 2001 by the economist Jim O'Neill from the Goldman Sachs Bank – it referred to the countries which then were expected to be the world's most dominant economic powers by 2050. Later on the S for South Africa was added to the original acronym.

PART 1:

Imagining the World Cup

1.

'Imagine in the World Cup' — sport mega events and social exclusion in Brazil.

"Brazil is not for beginners"
(Antonio Carlos Jobim)

In June 2013, Brazil hosted the FIFA Confederations Cup. This event was meant to be a test for the country which would take the centre stage of the sporting world in forthcoming years: notably FIFA's World Cup in 2014 and the IOC's Olympic and Paralympic Games in 2016.

However, an occasion supposed to showcase to the world a new and well-developed country with modern sports facilities also displayed much more than the amazing football-art played by the victorious Brazilian team. The international press was faced with the spectacle of thousands of protesters marching down the country's streets.

The analysis by the then FIFA President, Sepp Blatter, of the protests — "everything will settle down when the football starts" — proved to be totally wrong: the public dissent gained strength during the competition as street protesters marched towards the stadiums and put forward several demands to politicians, mostly focused on social justice exigencies.

I am Brazilian by way of nationality and culture. Despite living in Australia since 2009 I closely follow Brazil's social life. I see how futebol continues to be central to the country's life. It is 'much more than a game' for Brazilians. As an Australian-based 'insider', I became astonished to observe what was taking place inside the new stadiums built in Brazil for the Confederations Cup and the 2014 World Cup.

These issues, which appear on the field but stem mostly from off-field issues, have a direct connection with the country's current social and political life. These led me to a profound, though seemingly paradoxical question: would futebol in Brazil survive the World Cup? As futebol represents one of the main spaces for social cohesion in the country, my real concern was about the survival of the country's cultural and social life under the new conditions imposed by global sport events such as the World Cup and, two years later, the Rio Olympics.

On the field, the Brazilian team looked good and won the 2013 Confederations Cup. Supporters were proud with the high-level commitment to the 'magical yellow jersey' displayed by the players. The team appeared to have exactly what Brazilians love: a mix of friendship, football-art and devotion.

It was a pleasant surprise for everyone that, in only a few months, the new coach Luis Felipe Scolari could inspire a totally positive spirit in the team – and Brazilians were the champions again! Nobody expected that, just one year later, the team would look dreadful and trashed by Germany.

However, off the field things were not that good. The stadiums and also the audience that attended the Confederations Cup games revealed a country where, despite the big economic and social advances that took place in the first decade of the 2000s, the social inequality was still massive – and perhaps it was growing.

Watching the new modern and comfortable stadiums (the so-called 'arenas') on TV I was shocked: I asked myself where is that competition being played? Where were the stadiums where I used to go and cheer? The stadiums looked all the same!

They could be in Recife, in Salvador or Rio – but also in Sydney or London!

The 'FIFA-standard' had imposed an awful homogeneity, a '21st century' stadiums experience that had destroyed the cultural meanings and the heritage of the Brazilian stadiums.

The internationally eminent Maracanã stadium is the best example of this cultural heritage destruction. Maracanã was a public stadium built for the 1950 World Cup, when Brazil lost the final game against Uruguay, in the legendary 'Maracanazo'. As the Brazilian historian Burlamaqui Soares states, at that time the stadium was built with the clear intention of being a public space where all social classes were welcome. Maracanã had famous cheap spots (USD$5) where the most humble and poor supporters could cheer on their beloved team by standing on their feet behind the goals, following the games with their ears glued to their small radios.

These general admission cheap spots (in Portuguese, they were called 'geral' and their users known as 'Geraldinos') were an integral part of the stadium mythology; 'Geraldinos' have been portrayed in countless movies and stories.

With the renovations and the privatization of the stadium, though, the 'Geraldinos' disappeared, as the geral was simply destroyed, along with other symbols and heritage of the stadium. This 'modernisation' clearly showed that, in the Maracanã's new order there was no space for that ludic spectacle where everybody could participate.

The era of commercialised football arrived and the new owners look for customers with a 'new profile' – VIPs who could pay expensive tickets and spent a lot of money inside the stadium. One of the few leisure spaces for the Brazilian 'Geraldinos' was gone forever.

The concern with the standardised stadiums came along with another worry: the whitening of the audience during the Confederations Cup. Everyone who watched the Brazilian team playing could see that more than a half of the players are black or mulattos, which is a fair representation of a country where African descendants are the majority of the population.

On the grandstands, however, an international spectator who did not know much about Brazil would think that this is a country of white people. The absence of black/mulattos on the stands was remarkable – a clear sign of the economic and social exclusion that, together with the new stadiums, the World Cup imposes on the country.

Non-government organisations that represent the Brazilian African descendants had unsuccessfully demanded quotas during the years that preceded the World Cup inside the stadiums to allow the humble Brazilians (black/mulattos in the greater part) who worship the National team to attend the World Cup games.

As soon as Brazil was nominated to be the host of the 2014 World Cup, people on the streets, when complaining about daily life – such as heavy traffic, overcrowded hospitals and public transport, robberies, violence and corruption – started to say the mantra 'imagine in the World Cup'. This was the ironic way that Brazilians express their frustration and shame: if things currently are tough, can you 'imagine in the World Cup'? It would be worse.

The whitening and elitism of the stadiums were 'imagine in the World Cup' affairs. They clearly indicated why Brazilians took over the streets to protest against the current social order. Violence and social inequity increased in the country, while day-to-day living conditions were in decline. It was hard to believe that facing so many social problems, billions of dollars of public money were spent on a World Cup for VIP people – which is also threatening the Brazilian way of living and experiencing one of its most precious cultural symbols, futebol.

One year before the start of the competition, the legacy of the 2014 World Cup to the country was already controversial. One point, however, was clear: unlike futebol where everybody stands, cheers and play together, the World Cup would not increase social cohesion amongst Brazilians; on the contrary, it would intensify social exclusion.

Hence the central question that came to the mind of the lovers of authentic Brazilian football was just one: would Brazilian futebol survive the 2014 FIFA World Cup and in the future assist again, as it did in the past, with the process of including in public life the millions of Brazilians who were and still are socially disenfranchised?

After all, the World Cup may be FIFA's – but futebol will forever be Brazilian!

2.

Screw the World Cup
— but call me if the Seleção scores, please!

My earliest and fondest World Cup memories are from the Mexico tournament in 1970. I was only a toddler, but I remember helping my family decorate the house and streets with national symbols and colours. I have a clear recollection that after every win of the magic team led by Pelé, Tostão and the rest, we sketched Brazilian flags and went to festive street marches to celebrate.

After the unforgettable 4-1 win in the final against Italy at Azteca Stadium, I clearly recall sitting on my dad's lap, beeping the car horn while driving through the São Paulo streets to celebrate our *Seleção*.

Seleção is what we Brazilians call our national football team. There are several Seleções in Brazil, of course: the basketball team, the volleyball team, or even the women's football *Seleção*. However, 'the' *Seleção* is only one: our male national football team, the nation's pride, the five-time world champions. It is the motherland in football boots.

In 1970, Brazil was under a military dictatorship. General Médici ruled during the most repressive period of this dictatorship. From 1969 to 1974, censorship, kidnapping, torture, disappearance and killing of government opponents were widespread in the underworld of the secret police and the army.

Médici's authoritarian regime extinguished the urban and rural guerrilla. Carlos Marighella, one of the most prominent guerrilla leaders in Brazil, was murdered on São Paulo's streets in 1969 during Médici's reign.

Médici was a bloody dictator who used the *Seleção* to hide his evil regime. Anecdotal stories have it that he was a football lover and had a great knowledge of the game. Pictures of Médici with a small battery radio glued to his ear are part of the nation's football psyche. The military used the popularity of the national team to make propaganda of their undemocratic political regime. The *Seleção* had to go to Brasilia before and after its successful Mexican journey. The pictures of the players alongside Médici made the headlines of all main newspapers of the period, which were under heavy censorship by the army rulers.

In the course of the 'leaden years' (the most repressive period of the military dictatorship, from 1968 to 1974), many radical opponents of the dictatorial government – including Dilma Rousseff who was President of Brazil from 2011 to 2016 – went underground to participate in the guerrilla movements which fought the military rule.

Aware that the authoritarian government was making political use of the *Seleção*, the guerrilla leaders made a decision. All insurgents would cheer against the *Seleção*; they wouldn't comply to or help the regime's propaganda.

However, during the matches something different happened. Fernando Gabeira, a former guerrilla who participated in the kidnapping of the US Ambassador to Brazil, Charles Elbrick, in 1969 tells how the guerrillas were conflicted in his acclaimed book, O *que é isso, Companheiro?* (What the hell, mate?).

Gabeira says that the guerillas assembled in front of the TV, quiet, watching a *Seleção* match, having firmly decided to support the opposition. But as soon as Pelé scored a goal, they couldn't help but celebrate. Feelings towards the *Seleção* were stronger even than their political will.

Celebrating the World Cup (a 'Copa') and the *Seleção* is a cultural tradition embedded in Brazilians' lives. Every four years, a few months before the tournament kicks off, people start to decorate the streets with the national colours, flags and street art to cheer on the team. Party arrangements are made.

The main question that everybody asks is: where are you going to watch the match? Even those who don't enjoy football take advantage of the official and unofficial holidays on *Seleção* match days to at least rest. When the *Seleção* plays in the World Cup, the country stops. Bank branches, schools, universities, courts – they all close to watch 'the match'.

A few weeks before the World Cup, my dear friend Bill Murray came to Sydney to launch his most recent book, A *History of Football in Australia: A Game of Two Halves* (written with Roy Hay). While entertaining my family at dinner with his amazing football stories, Bill, also the author of *The World's Game: a History of Soccer*, told us that he spent the 1994 World Cup, hosted by the United States, in Rio de Janeiro!

Bill wanted to feel the famous Brazilian mood during the Copa. He said he had never seen anything like it. The parties and the street decoration were fantastic; the mood was good – and his time to do research was restricted, as the city library closed in the middle of the day.

In 2014, though, the mood on Brazil's streets before the World Cup was not the same. There was an anti-World Cup decoration 'movement'. The usual decorations only just popped up in the week prior to the tournament, and were not prominent. The joy of the World Cup was overshadowed with bitterness, revolt and anger.

Hosting the party at home made everything hard for Brazilians. The promise of the 'world's best party' gave rise to huge social justice demands, and the forced relocations of marginalised communities amidst human rights violations and allegations of huge corruption disturbed the celebrations. The 'people' did not comply with the idealised role the authorities had for them – singing and dancing. They went to the streets to protest.

Protests and strikes are not new in World Cup host countries. For example, a few days before the 1998 World Cup in France, Air France pilots went on strike against the company's proposed salaries cuts.

However, things were worse in Brazil and among several, spontaneous protests, the Homeless Worker's Association (MTST) decided to act. The MTST is one of the most organised and organic social movements in Brazil. Since 1997 it has fought for urban reform aimed at giving back the cities to the marginalised people.

In May 2014, the MTST occupied an abandoned area close to the Itaquerão Stadium in São Paulo, where the World Cup opening ceremony occurred. Ironically, MTST members named that occupation the 'Copa do Povo', the 'people's World Cup'. Just a few days before the start of the tournament, the well-organised activists marched towards the Itaquerão Stadium. 20,000 protesters closed the stadium's surrounding streets with a clear message: if the government did not listen to them, they would stop the opening ceremony.

After months of procrastination and lack of dialogue, the federal government quickly made a decision. As per the MTST's demands, they included the whole association in the national housing program, 'My House My Life'. The MTST leaders celebrated that achievement as a 'people's victory'. They promised not to disturb the opening ceremony.

On the other hand, the São Paulo state government used its well-known heavy hand to silence the subway workers' strike before the world tournament. The state government commands one of the most violent military police forces in the country, and has made little progress to open a dialogue with the subway workers on strike, who were demanding not only better wages but also safer work conditions.

São Paulo's state government still faces serious corruption allegations in the construction of the São Paulo city's subway network, which is the largest in the country and provides connections to the train and busses network too.

Protests occurred even in the week of the opening ceremony. A huge street demonstration occurred while the *Seleção* was playing its final warm-up match against Serbia. Protesters were angry, but stopped protesting for a while to celebrate the sole goal of the match, scored by Fred.

Brazilian feminist activist Sandra Unbehaum used a metaphor to explain the mood on the streets. For her, the moment is like when you're hosting a huge party at your house, but just minutes before your visitors arrive, your partner comes to you and says he wants a divorce. In other words, during the event you have to pretend nothing has happened, but the fact is you can't enjoy anything.

On the other hand, Unbehaum also says that the Brazilian tradition of the World Cup sticker album had really spread across the country. On weekends, children, teenagers and adults assembled close to the newsagencies to buy and swap players' stickers. It was a moment of bliss.

Brazilian people's feelings were mixed just before the event's starting moment. The way the World Cup was managed brought anger and bitterness mixed with joy and happiness. Authorities made sure that the host cities were well-protected: nobody has ever seen such a huge contingent of police, army and private security in Brazil's cities.

Before the opening ceremony, federal ministers and even the president were on TV every day to assure Brazilians that this World Cup would be the best ever.

With just a few hours to go, I was anxious, as were my fellow Brazilians. I was afraid that something bad would occur on the streets or during the opening ceremony.

All ended up working well.

Ever since Brazil won the hosting rights 2007, I had mixed feelings towards the event. I didn't agree with the process that those in charge put together to organise the event. But I couldn't help joining in and cheering on the *Seleção*. It is a familiar story now with fans as we prepare for the 2018 World Cup. Although the entire 2018/2022 World Cup bidding contest is universally acknowledged as being corrupt, it doesn't take away from the football once it starts.

So here I was, half-way around the world, waking up really early in the morning in Australia to watch every match of my beloved national team – but with an eye on the streets.

Viva the *Seleção*!

3.

The game owners:
a brief history of the Teixeira-Havelange famiglia

The football world has many stories of sons who have followed their fathers' footballing steps. Some have had success, others haven't. In Italy, both Maldinis (the dad Cesare and the son Paolo) conquered the hearts of Milan FC supporters. In France, Youry and Jean Djorkaeff shone wearing 'Les Bleus' jersey. More recently, the Zidanes (Luca and Enzo) are also following the steps of their famous father, Zinedine.

There are also stories that show that genetics is not the only feature that a son needs to follow in his father's successful football career: Pelé's son Edinho, after a few seasons as an average goalkeeper for Santos FC, ended up in jail accused of association with drug dealers.

João Havelange and Ricardo Teixeira produced one of the most famous 'daddy and son' off-field associations in the football world. Even though the notorious duo of footballing 'big-shots' were not linked by any genetic ties, they were like father and son. The 'father' passed to the 'son' a curious inheritance: the appetite for powerful positions in the sports world.

Havelange, who reigned over the former National Sports Council (CND) from 1957 to 1974 and was FIFA's president from 1974 to 1988, never had a son of his own. Hence, in 1973 when his daughter Lucia married Ricardo Teixeira, he became, in Havelange's word, "the son I never had". In fact, prior to giving birth to their only child, Havelange's wife lost two boys due to complications in her pregnancies. Thus, Teixeira not only occupied a 'son's place' in Havelange's heart; his bond with his father-in-law turned out to be more intense and enduring than the marital relationship with Havelange's daughter.

Born in 1926 as Jean-Marie Faustin Godefroid Havelange in Rio de Janeiro, he was raised in an old-fashioned manner and his first language was French. Havelange tried to be a footballer and even played as a defender for Fluminense in 1931. However, Faustin, his father, was a conservative Belgian man, who disliked football and pushed his son to give up on football and to become an elite swimmer, a sport more aligned with his social standing.

Two years after his father's death, Havelange travelled to Germany and competed in the 1936 Berlin Games as a swimmer. He did not win a medal, but has always declared his profound admiration for the 'Nazi Olympics', considered by him as "one of the greatest shows I have ever seen in my life; everything was magnificent, the organisation was perfect, they paid attention to every detail."

Havelange was a strong swimming competitor. It was in this time that Havelange learned not only how to navigate and survive in rivers and pools, but also how to compete and be successful in more obscure waters: that of sports politics.

His career as sports administrator started at the São Paulo Swimming Federation in 1948, while still an athlete. He headed this sports body until 1951 and since then did not cease involvement with sporting institutions until 2015, one year before his death at age 99. He participated as a water-polo athlete-director in the 1951 Buenos Aires Pan-American Games – where he declared his admiration for another authoritarian political leader, Juan Domingo Peron. In the same double role, he went to the 1952 Helsinki Olympic Games to become director of Aquatic Sports at the Brazilian Sports Council (CND). He brokered several deals that paved his way to the top position of this Council. In 1957, his election as president of the CND was the beginning of the Havelange Era in world sport.

Anecdotal sources state that Havelange did not enjoy football, which might not be entirely true. However, he enjoyed much more the power and the money that came from his positions within the football bodies. During his administration, the *Seleção* won the 1958 Sweden and the 1962 Chile World Cups. Havelange did not travel to either of these tournaments. To lead the team abroad he sent Paulo Machado de Carvalho, an influential football politician from São Paulo. They talked over the phone every two days, so Havelange was kept informed about the team, while receiving sponsors and political authorities in his Rio de Janeiro office.

Havelange was always a master in using football as a means to build good connections with people in powerful positions. After the 1964 army coup d'état, he quickly constructed good relations with the ruling military and happily accepted their nominations for the commanding positions within the victorious 1970 *Seleção*. On the other hand, the military knew how influential Havelange was within the sports world and tried to keep him under their radar.

The military were happy with the distraction that the 1970 Mexico World Cup win offered to their fascist and violent political regime. Thus, with the Jules Rimet trophy on his hands and the key to the CND's safe box in his pocket, Havelange enlarged his ambitions and started to pursue FIFA's top-seat.

Havelange knew that in order to be elected to FIFA's presidency, he needed the votes of non-European countries, so he used the major card that he had close to his chest: Pelé. The planet's most popular footballer was venerated in African and Asian countries. Employing Pelé as his ambassador both travelled around the world for two years, building up all the needed political connections within the footballing federations worldwide.

Havelange always maintained that he used his own money to pay for all the travelling. However, after visiting nearly 100 countries during his political campaign, CND's bank accounts were in severe debt; and Pelé's financial troubles and debts had disappeared.

CND's funds also paid for the *Seleção's* international excursions during that period. As the reigning World champions, the team did not need to compete in the tournament qualifiers so Havelange arranged for the team to play in Algiers and in Tunis.

Havelange's last hurdle was conquering Adidas, FIFA's major commercial partner. Again using the services of Pelé, he approached Adidas' owner Horst Dassler, who was following Havelange political movements and who wanted to meet the 'football king'. Stanley Rous, then FIFA's president, did not notice Havelange's smart political tactics. In July 1974, with Adidas as his ally, Havelange was elected as FIFA's president.

In the meanwhile, the Brazilian army was unhappy with Havelange because he could not convince Pelé to interrupt his retirement and play again for the *Seleção* in the 1974 Germany World Cup. Moreover, he left a huge financial debt at the CND's banks accounts. To avoid an international scandal, the military decided to cover the debts Havelange left in the CND's bank account; in return Havelange, who wanted to keep both positions at CND and FIFA, was forced to leave the former.

At FIFA, Havelange used his aggressive political and commercial practices – which were denounced along the years by many journalists – to build an empire. He was never happy to be pushed away from Brazilian football though, and waited with patience for the right moment to come back to his original kingdom.

In 1979, following FIFA's guidelines that each country-member should have a football-exclusive body, the CND was extinguished and the Brazilian Football Confederation (CBF) was created. During the ensuing years, Brazilian football was immersed in a huge crisis: the *Seleção* had not won a title since 1970, and within Brazil, football was enduring severe financial and political troubles.

In the mid-1980s, the CBF faced significant management issues and did not have the administrative structure in place to organise a national domestic championship; hence in 1987 a Club's League was formed to do so. Havelange, who was patiently seating in his FIFA's throne waiting since 1974 to reign again over Brazilian football, knew that his moment had arrived.

Aware of this leadership vacuum in the CBF, he started to lobby on behalf of his family. He presented his son-in-law to the Brazilian football authorities as a savvy and modern administrator who would save Brazilian football.

Using his well-known aggressive tactics, Havelange's lobbying was victorious. In 1989, Ricardo Teixeira, a man who had no idea about football, was elected as president of the CBF. Teixeira was soon to show that he had learnt all the lessons about 'modern' football management from his father-in-law.

Unknown players connected to powerful agents were soon to be called to the *Seleção* line-up, and then sold to international clubs for undeclared prices. However, Teixeira's master move was waiving the CBF's rights to receive any public money from the sports betting lotteries which were funding national sporting bodies. This refusal reinforced the CBF's profile as a private entity that could not be prosecuted for misuse of taxpayer's money.

Moreover, under Havelange's supervision, Teixeira used football and the *Seleção* to construct a powerful empire of obscure transactions. He created several companies moving money around different countries. He signed suspicious sponsorship contracts. His political methods were totally authoritarian.

As CBF's president, Teixeira became a wealthy man. His dark commercial deals led to a National Parliamentary Inquiry about CBF's practices in the early 2000s. Despite the evidence that a few independent national parliamentary representatives had against him, the inquiry had no practical consequences and its final report was censored.

The Brazilian tradition says that when a child is born, s/he receives two family names. The first name (the 'middle' name) is the mother's maiden surname. The last and most important name is the father's surname, which is passed to the next generation.

Teixeira changed this custom and used his children to reinforce his ties with Joao Havelange. Despite the usual tradition which would dictate that Ricardo Teixeira's offspring should be called 'Havelange Teixeira', all Havelange's grandchildren were named as 'Teixeira Havelange'. The son-in-law-who-was-like-a-son knew that the grandfather's heart would be pleased to have his name well-looked-after for future generations.

Hence, Teixeira's ties with his father-in-law were shaken but not destroyed when Havelange's daughter divorced him. The reason for the split was that Teixeira was caught in a love affair with a younger woman who subsequently passed away in a car accident in Florida.

Havelange and Teixeira's famiglia bonds were only affected when the first outcomes of several investigations into FIFA's corrupt transactions started to appear. In 2012, after a deal with the Court authorities in Zug, Switzerland, both had to pay back a substantial sum to the authorities to avoid further prosecution. They also quietly stepped away from their positions at FIFA and at the IOC. Teixeira was also forced to renounce his position as CBF's president and World Cup local Organising committee chair, and left Brazil to live in his mansion in Miami.

Joana Havelange, Teixeira's daughter from his first marriage to Lucia, kept the position his father arranged for her within the 2014 World Cup local Organising committee even after her father's resignation. Her luxury life remained intact as she boasted of her overseas trips and expensive purchases on her social media channels.

She did not realize that the country's social context was changing. She even posted a pearl on her social media channels just a few months before the competition: "Everything that was to be stolen for the World Cup already has been; let's try to make a good tournament".

That post went viral. Joana seemed to be incapable of perceiving that the nation was tired of the amount of corruption and social injustice that was being broadcast every single day.

The street demonstrations that had shaken the country on the eve of FIFA's tournaments did not disturb her lifestyle. She just wanted to proceed with World Cup business as usual.

The chaotic social scenario, the fire aimed at her own local Organising committee from the local press and the public, the corruption accusations and demands for social justice and against FIFA that abounded on every corner of the country – nothing appeared to bother Teixeira's daughter and Havelange's granddaughter.

She wanted the public to overlook the corruption and just enjoy the tournament.

Did she simply forget that her father was in the top of the list of people accused of misuse of public money and corruption in the Brazil World Cup? Or, just as her powerful dad, she just did not care?

It looks like, that in this case, the footballing genetics were well-transmitted from father to daughter.

4.

Pelé and Ronaldo:
from national pride to anti heroes

Sporting culture has countless heroes across the world. The universal sports pantheon has plenty of (super) women and men who fulfil the role of heroine or hero for nearly every nation. The global hall of fame has stories that go from epic athletic performances that reached the pinnacle of sporting success, to physical demonstrations that, even when not achieving gold, show the fibre of a particular culture and are celebrated by that country.

Brazil is no different. The country has plenty of heroes and heroines to display in its sports hall of fame, such as the Formula 1 driver Ayrton Senna, basketballers Paula and Hortencia, or the twice Olympic gold medallist triple jumper, Adhemar Ferreira da Silva.

However, it is mostly on the football field where heroes have been created and adored by generations of Brazilians. Of course, at the top of this list, far above everyone, shines Pelé, the 20th century athlete and the only man to have won the FIFA World Cup three times as a player.

A few steps below him, but still at a high point, is the Phenomenon named Ronaldo Nazario, the striker who represented Brazil in four World Cups and scored 67 goals for the national team (15 during World Cups). Ronaldo was also involved in many controversies while wearing the sacred *Seleção's* mantle, but finally delivered a title to the country in 2002, which was the fifth and last time that Brazil has seen the *Seleção* winning a world title.

Both Pelé and Ronaldo came from humble origins and from society's margins, but they made it to the top level of sport, accumulating fortunes and being admired, courted and envied by the powerful across many nations, including presidents and kings. Their social rise from nowhere makes their story more appealing to the national imagination. They deservedly achieved the status of heroes in Brazil because of their footballing efforts and achievements.

Parents have been using their examples for decades to try to inspire their offspring to achieve their footballing goals. They are praised in every sporting scenario and in countless narratives of their on-field prowess. And they are much adored by the country's more socially vulnerable communities who see these players as their inspiration. Pelé and Ronaldo appear to be sacred figures who were so revered that it was as if they should not be questioned in anyway.

Nevertheless, as their careers in and around football continued after they hung-up their boots, controversies started to surround them.

Pelé, whose footballing career achieved its apex during the military dictatorship, has always been pressured by the left-wing intelligentsia to take on board the necessities of the poorest and to be a leader of anti-racism campaigns in particular.

A few scenarios would be perfect for him to stand out for the 'people's rights'. Even as a player, he could have assumed this role. For example, in the November 1969 game against Vasco da Gama, he converted a penalty shot late at night (23h30) at the end of the match to score his 1,000th goal.

In a Maracanã packed with more than 65,000 supporters, and with the whole press having their eyes on him, he asked that Brazilians should think on and look after the 'poorer children' as Christmas was arriving and they needed more attention. That cannot be deemed as a revolutionary speech, nor was it something that would challenge the anti-democratic government of that time. However, it was indicative of what Pelé could produce on that day.

He never argued against the country's authorities or the political establishment. Nobody can also imagine what would have happened to him if he had assumed a confrontational position against the establishment during the darkest years of the military dictatorship.

As much as the left-wing intelligentsia would have enjoyed having Pelé as their activist for several social causes, he has never been a man who used his celebrity status to advance a social agenda.

Pelé even created two public personas and always refers to them by using the third person: he talks about Pelé the player and Edson (his first name), the citizen. As many point out, Pelé was a king and Edson is a human being with plenty of contradictions and faults.

Yet, he has had access to the circles of power, and not only as a player who was used by Havelange to conquer votes in the Brazilian's quest to become FIFA's president. Many years later, Pelé continued to have a highly prestigious name within high society, being nominated as the Federal Minister of Sports during Fernando Henrique Cardoso's presidency (1995-2002). He remained in this position for four years and while there he advanced laws to protect professional footballers in Brazil (the Pelé bill).

Ronaldo was also adored as a player. There is a joke amongst Brazilian journalists that no bad news would ever stick to Ronaldo. A potentially inflammatory story brings some evidence to this view.

In 2008 he was picked-up by police at dawn in one of Rio de Janeiro's notoriously bad streets, allegedly dealing drugs with some professional transvestites. The news made the TV and the main newspapers but quickly disappeared from the headlines, with no affect on his career or his position as a national hero.

Ten years prior to that, during the final moments of the 1998 France World Cup, he was the central character of another episode that could have badly damaged his career and his image. But he escaped this incident unharmed and with his heroic persona strengthened. Ronaldo suffered a health crisis on the night before the final match against France. He allegedly had a seizure on his room that was witnessed by other players. The whole team was panicking and the atmosphere was tense in the *Seleção*'s headquarters. Ronaldo spent the hours prior to the game in a French hospital, undertaking several medical examinations, including CAT scans.

Zagallo, then the *Seleção*'s coach, fearing for Ronaldo's health, did not include him in the initial list of the starting 11 players. As soon as that list went public, Teixeira went down to the team's changing room to demand Ronaldo's inclusion in the starting team.

Pushed by Teixeira, Zagallo changed his mind and included Ronaldo in the starting 11. The players' group was dissatisfied about this last minute change. There were rumours of an incipient fist fight among a small numbers of players that many consider contributed to the team's defeat in that final game.

There were many conspiracy theories about Nike's role in that decision also. Ronaldo was not only a Nike sponsored footballer, but the company was also one of the major sponsors of the CBF. For many, it was not hard to join the dots and come up with the theory that Nike wanted 'their' man to play.

After the France World Cup, the main Brazilian TV broadcasters spent countless hours talking about Ronaldo's crisis. Medical specialists were interviewed. Round tables were organised. Nevertheless, most of the comments about him in the mainstream media channels were positive. His bravery to play the final under such distress was commended and it helped pave his way to the top of the Brazilian sports heroes' pantheon.

But among several controversies that both Pelé and Ronaldo participated in throughout their lives, one has marked their respective public persona forever: their pronouncements during the widespread street demonstrations that took place in the eve of the 2013 Confederations Cup in Brazil.

While people were occupying the streets protesting against many social issues in the country, including against FIFA's demands over the World Cup facilities and its costly standards; while FIFA officials, players and media workers (counting Pelé and Ronaldo among them) could not leave their luxury, secure accommodation due to unrest in the streets; while street banners demanded better public education and health, Ronaldo declared that "nobody does a World Cup with hospitals, we need good stadiums."

Pelé's words were no better. He acknowledged that people on the streets were unhappy due to the many allegations of corruption around FIFA and the CBF, but he still asked for the demonstrators to go home, as "the corrupt already stole everything they could; please, let's make a beautiful party [for the World Cup] so tourists will come and we'll recover this money."

Despite these polemics, Pelé and Ronaldo will forever be preserved as national heroes. Their great sporting achievements, though, were not enough to erase the prevalent racism against black people within Brazilian society. As a master of public relations, Ronaldo has been well whitened on his way to the top, from his hair, to his body and smile. Pelé, who is irrefutably black, was once deemed to be a 'black with a white soul', hence acceptable to mainstream Brazilian society.

Enduring structural racism may have blocked these heroes to build a public consciousness and to use their fame to help advancing social justice in the country.

Brazilian football is yet to conceive its equivalent of Nelson Mandela.

5.

Romário: the striker at the national Parliament

The year is 2002. Luiz Felipe Scolari, then in his first term as the *Seleção*'s coach, is about to announce the final squad for the 2002 World Cup. The list dominates the country's imagination, from everyday conversations in schools, pubs, streets and workplaces, to all media outlets. Nobody seems to be talking about anything else.

Brazilian money is declining in comparison to the US dollar? A leftist candidate is ahead in the polls for that year's presidential elections? Nobody cares. The central question is: will Romário survive the final cut and make it to what would be his last chance to play in a World Cup final?

Just one day before Scolari's announcement, 'Shorty' (as Romário was affectionately nicknamed by his friends and the press) called a media conference. In front of the major Brazilian broadcasters, wearing a T-shirt and unshaven, he appeals to the coach to call him. Romário insists that he would not mind being on the team's bench as the most important part was that with his experience, he could make a valuable contribution to the national team for the last time in his playing career. Tears dropped down his face. Everyone was moved.

Except Scolari. For the past two days, he could not be found anywhere and by nobody. He watched the interview in his hiding place, only accompanied by his always loyal assistant coach, Murtosa. He had already made his mind up about Romário and was hiding to avoid all the pressure from the streets, the press and mostly from the Brazilian Federation 'owner', Ricardo Teixeira who had promised Shorty that he would be in the 2002 World Cup.

According to Romário, Teixeira repeatedly said to him that he was the boss and Scolari would have to call Shorty to the World Cup. The next day, when the squad was announced at CBF's headquarters, Romário was not nominated. On that day, Teixeira was not in his office. Left alone in the CBF's headquarters, Scolari had to deal with the media lions who were arguing for Shorty to be included.

Scolari had to leave the building by a back door to escape from angry Romário supporters. Many years later, Scolari declared that Romário's final interview touched his heart and he nearly changed his mind. But then he recalled other media performances of the player, and decided that the interview was just an act. The *Seleção* went to Asia and lifted the 2002 title without Shorty.

Twelve years later, a well-shaved short man with some grey hair, wearing a tailored dark suit and a pink tie, went to the country's Senate tribune.

Romário, just elected as Senator by Rio de Janeiro state constituents, delivers his first speech in his new position. In the prior Parliamentary term, he was already a federal representative, but this time he made a larger step to climb further up the political ladder. He wants everyone to acknowledge his progression.

In the tribune, he gloats about the more than four million votes that he received, making him the most voted Senator in Rio's history. He proclaims his pride in his poor heritage, stating that it's not that often that someone from a *favela* (slum) gets elected to the federal Senate. He continues by declaring that he might not be the most experienced Senator, and that he is just starting his political career, but he has supreme life experiences that only people who grew up in misery would have.

He paints himself in opposition to the majority of the Senators who were born in a gold cradle. They would never understand the feelings of a poor child, on the verge of starvation, and having to walk several miles to school each day, as he did not have money to take a bus. His family had no fridge or other basic facilities at his home. He was born and raised as a *favelado* (slum's inhabitant). In no moment of his four-minute introductory speech does he mention his position as a former football star. As soon as he leaves the lectern, the chairman of the session acknowledges his football skills, by comparing his goals on the fields to the future goals he would score as a Senator.

Romário was one of the finest strikers that world football has ever seen. He played for the major Brazilian clubs such as Vasco da Gama and Flamengo, and also for Netherlands' PSV Eindhoven and, for two seasons, Barcelona in Spain. He was the first of a streak of Brazilian attackers who would thrill Barcelona's fans over several decades, followed by Rivaldo, Ronaldo, Ronaldinho Gaúcho and Neymar.

He is the *Seleção*'s third top-scorer, with 55 goals, just below Pelé and Ronaldo, but his goal average is greater than both. Major South American football magazines such as the Argentinean El Grafico considers him the world's greatest scorer with 768 goals in official matches (Pelé counts goals as a junior player and in friendlies as well to reach more than 1,000 goals scored).

Placar, another eminent Brazilian football magazine, matches his goals scoring numbers to Pelé's numbers, giving 720 goals to each in official matches. Other evidence of Romário's excellence as football player include being the golden boot winner in 27 out of 83 official competitions he played in, and being named the best player in the world in the 1994 FIFA awards.

Romário was also controversial as a player. He was one of a handful of players who wore the jersey of Rio de Janeiro's three major clubs

(Vasco da Gama, Flamengo and Fluminense). He was adored by all their supporters and hated by their managers who frequently did not pay his wages and were sued by him. At the end of his career, he missed plenty of training sessions to be found playing *futevolei* – a game that combines the skills of football on a volleyball court which is highly popular on Brazilian beaches – on Copacabana beach. A professional football club even started to organise training sessions on the beach so Romário could attend them.

On his final days as a professional footballer (in the mid-2000s), with several physical issues and clearly out of shape, he still managed to score dozens of goals and, at 39 years old, he was the golden boot winner of the 2005 Brazilian Championship scoring 22 goals. He did not run at all, but he had a striker's 'killer instinct' in the penalty box and could always make his mark.

If Romário was an extremely lazy player in his final playing years, he proved to be the opposite in his early years as politician.

Prior to his election as Senator, but already in Brasilia as a Congressman, Romário engaged in several working parties related to sports, education and disability issues. He presented draft legislation on these themes, and was a severe critic of the CBF, pointing out the sporting body's corrupt practices.

Romário took advantage of the Brazilian parliamentary tradition, where not only the party leaders but any Senator can ask to step on the stage to argue about any issue. In his first term Romário went to the stage nearly 50 times to deliver speeches about the need for better education in the country. He also demanded more sports programs related to healthy lifestyles and for improved support services for people with a disability.

He also frequently voiced his concerns about the 2014 FIFA World Cup tainted practices and other corrupt sporting bodies. He even collected enough support to open a Parliamentary Inquiry into the Federation's wrongdoings – which was later blocked by the chairman, who was a CBF ally.

As a Senator, Romário continued his battles against degraded practices within the sports realm. However, as a newcomer in this playing field, he showed that he started to learn his new game's rules.

When the crucial bill to impeach the elected president Dilma Roussef came to the Senate in 2016, Romário, who represented a party that was a former ally to the president, was about to vote 'no'. However, after some behind-the-scenes deals, he left the Senate Ethics committee which was analysing Roussef's situation and his final vote was pro-impeachment of the Roussef.

Romário seems to be as fast in the Senate as he was in the penalty box.

6.

Never say no to Teixeira: famiglia business and the new World Cup stadiums

FIFA considered that eight luxurious stadiums would be more than enough for Brazil to successfully host the World Cup. However, the Local Organising Committee, supported by the Federal Government, decided that Brazil would have 12 host cities. The history involving the twelve stadiums that were renovated or built for the 2014 World Cup deserves a Netflix series of their own. It would reveal, episode after episode, all the characters involved in the intrigues that led to the choice of the host cities and the stadiums building process.

Brazil has 27 states and nearly every state wanted to build a new stadium and host at least a few games of the World Cup group stage or even the tournament's knock-out phases. Lula, the then president of Brazil, personally negotiated with Teixeira, the CBF's president, who was also the chairman of the World Cup Local Organising Committee. Lula also discussed with politicians and business people from around the country, to finally agree on the 12 cities that would host the World Cup.

Yet, in the case of a few cities such as São Paulo which, given its political, economic and sporting status was a certain candidate to host important World Cup matches, the decision was even tougher. Should the city just renovate an already existing stadium (Morumbi) as stated in Brazil's World Cup bid documentation, or should it build a totally new stadium from scratch?

This decision involved several characters and a complex footballing political chess game. It began in 1987 when a sporting body called *Clube dos* 13 (the Club of the 13) was founded. As previously noted, at that time, Brazilian football administration was a mess and the CBF could not organise a national championship. Hence, the Clube dos 13 was born to protect the political and economic interests of the country's biggest clubs, such as Flamengo, São Paulo, Grêmio, Cruzeiro, Bahia, Fluminense and others.

A few years later, this elite group expanded to include other clubs bringing it to a total of 20 teams. The Clube dos 13 main role was to negotiate sponsorships and broadcasting deals on behalf of its members. A few times, though, the Clube dos 13 organised the national championship on behalf of the CBF.

A few years after the founding of Clube dos 13, the Havelange-Teixeira famiglia returned as Brazilian's football central power. As the new CBF president, Ricardo Teixeira was assiduous in building a strong network of political and economic connections among politicians and judges in the federal spheres, as well as to quickly growing his business empire.

Teixeira's connections were vital in protecting him during the parliamentary inquiries into the CBF that started in the early 2000s. There was always a free spot for Teixeira's influential partners to attend the *Seleção's* international matches, while enjoying the best hospitality that the world could provide as his guests.

As the history of the new Arena Corinthians built in São Paulo city for the World Cup will show, Teixeira always knew how to compensate his allies.

However, the Clube dos 13 was a football domain yet to be conquered by Teixeira and his famiglia.

Fabio Koff, the president of Grêmio Football Porto Alegrense, a founding team of the country's league was president of the Clube dos 13 since 1995. He had the support of the majority of the club members who were happy with Koff's way of conducting business.

Teixeira, though, could feel that a few clubs were dissatisfied with Koff's presidency and, in a political move to extend his already enormous power to the Clube dos 13, launched his ally, Kleber Leite, former Flamengo president, as the opposition candidate to the Clube dos 13 presidency. This political power struggle is the 'lost link' that connects all the characters involved in this drama to the São Paulo city World Cup stadium.

São Paulo Futebol Clube (SPFC) was the owner of the Morumbi stadium. For decades the SPFC's stadium was the only sports venue in the city able to host local and national derbies as well as major music events. The other major clubs in the city or in the state (such as Palmeiras, Corinthians and Santos) were usually forced to play their big matches in the SPFC stadium, reserving some of their ticket revenue to pay for the stadium lease. Hence, for many years, the stadium was a major source of capital for SPFC.

As the only major stadium in São Paulo city, Morumbi was meant to be renovated to host the 2014 World Cup opening game as well as other qualifying and knockout games in the tournament. Juvenal Juvêncio, then SPFC's president, already had stadium renovation plans and reportedly had the support of the city's, the state's, and even the country's authorities to go ahead with his ideas for the stadium to be a World Cup stadium. CBF and FIFA authorities visited the stadium and suggested some amendments to the renovation plans.

However, during the 2010 Clube dos 13 election, Juvenal Juvêncio picked the 'wrong' candidate. Loyal to his friend Fabio Koff, he went against Kleber Leite, then Teixeira's candidate. Leite (and Teixeira) lost that election but, silently, Teixeira got his revenge against Juvêncio and SPFC stadium.

Teixeira's first step was to implode the Clube dos 13 through an important ally, Andre Sanchez, then Corinthians president and also a member of Lula's workers party (PT). Sanchez, whose Corinthians – one of the most popular clubs in the country – never had a stadium, entered into a public dispute with Juvêncio, and broke his ties with the SPFC president.

At the same time, Sanchez endorsed Teixeira's candidate to the Clube dos 13 presidency. When Leite and Teixeira were defeated, Sanchez announced that the Corinthians were leaving the Clube dos 13 and would make their broadcasting arrangements individually. That was the start of a revolt within the Clube dos 13 as many clubs followed Corinthians' lead and organised their broadcasting deals without the central sporting body. In effect, the core activity of the Clube dos 13 suffered a mortal wound.

Sanchez would soon be rewarded for his loyalty to Teixeira.

Suddenly, FIFA started to identify several problems with the Morumbi's bid to host the World Cup.

The stadium candidature was slowly being eroded from diverse angles.

At the same time, a huge informal alliance was quickly formed to support the construction of a new stadium on the other side of the city, to be owned by Corinthians after the World Cup. This new coalition had the support of important people such as Sanchez, Teixeira, FIFA, local and state politicians and above all, the then country's president, Lula, who is a fanatical Corinthians supporter.

New lands were identified close to the Corinthians headquarters. This was in an impoverished area in the eastern suburbs of São Paulo city. A new line of investment was quickly opened by the Brazilian bank of economic and social development. The Arena Corinthians, which was long a dream of the Corinthians community, was becoming a reality. The new stadium was Sanchez's compensation for his loyalty towards Teixeira, as well as Teixeira's payback for Juvêncio's lack of support during the Clube dos 13 dispute.

Morumbi was out of the World Cup, and the Arena Corinthians would host the opening match.

However, as the World Cup was about to start, the Arena Corinthians faced a major challenge. One of the largest social movements in Brazil (the Landless Movement) launched a campaign to block São Paulo's streets on the verge of the World Cup. This was primarily to denounce several promises the government broke and to restate their demands for social justice. 30,000 of their members started to march towards the Arena Corinthians, threatening to destroy it and create chaos to interrupt the World Cup.

Rapidly, though, the social movement changed their direction and conducted their protests elsewhere.

The Arena was protected by the Corinthians' ultras known as the *Gaviões da Fiel* (the Loyal Hawks), one of the largest and more organised supporters' groups in the country. The Gaviões members did not care about the corrupt political arrangements that enabled the Arena to be built. They organised themselves through their social media channels and went down, armed with sticks and probably guns, to defend their new 'mansion' at all costs.

It was one of the rare moments in the World Cup when the people power helped to protect the interest of the powerful people.

7.

Following Sócrates' paths: Bom Senso FC and the start of a footballing revolt

I effortlessly recall that day in April 1984.

It was a warm autumn sunset in São Paulo, the largest and richest Brazilian city. I was one of almost two million people who marched in an enormous square known as *Vale do Anhagabaú*, situated in the heart of South America's most populated metropolis.

It was the leading rally of a social movement which had begun a year earlier and after a few months took the streets of all major and regional Brazilian cities. In all assemblies through the nation, the pacifist activists wore white head ribbons and carried signs and flags demanding 'free elections now!' We craved to elect our president, a civic right that was taken from us 20 years earlier by the 1964 military coup d'état.

This April 1984 demonstration in São Paulo was a vital one, as it was taking place only one week prior to the national Parliament gathering to vote for the bill that would permit free presidential elections once again. On the edge of the Vale do Anhagabaú it was possible to perceive a vast stage crammed with musicians, intellectuals, artists and politicians waiting their time to sing or speak. The official speakers of the day were left-wing traditional leaders who were expatriated during the military dictatorship, and who returned to the country after the 1979 Amnesty Law.

New political leaders such as Lula – the unionist who led the first massive workers' strikes in the course of the military government – were also scheduled to speak. Lula, who, 18 years later as elected president, commanded Brazil's World Cup bid. The same Lula, who was a football lover and a Corinthians fanatical supporter, was one of the most anticipated speakers of that night.

Another of the featured speakers on that historical night was Sócrates, one of Brazil's supreme players and also the leader of the Corinthians Democracy, a political football movement that took place in the country during 1982-83.

This movement, within one of the most popular Brazilian football clubs, requested that players' interests and opinions were heard during an era where there was no democracy in Brazil.

The demonstration was colourful. Resurgent political parties and social organizations that were banned during the dictatorship were strongly represented with their banners and partisans. Anxiety could definitely be felt in the atmosphere. Speakers representing various political opinions were hailed by their factions.

Yet, when Sócrates' turn to speak arrived, the crowd became quiet. As he was a tall man, it was possible to see him wearing a ribbon on his head between artists, journalists and politicians on the platform.

He did not speak for long. He simply declared his choice: if the bill was accepted, he would reject any millionaire offer from European teams and he would happily continue to play in what he thought would be a "new Brazil". Conversely, if the bill did not pass, he would leave the country to play in Italy. He would no more endure living in a non-democratic society.

Unfortunately for the country and for Sócrates' supporters, the bill did not pass. He went to Italy and Brazilians had to endure other five years of non-elected federal government until they finally could vote for president in 1989. However, Sócrates' actions left an enduring legacy.

Even prior to Sócrates and the Corinthians Democracy, social consciousness among players could be seen in Brazilian football. Since professional football started in the country (in the 1930s) Brazilian footballers had fought for their rights within a conformist and oppressive environment. In the early 1970s, Afonsinho, who played for Botafogo, protested against his manager and the club's Board as they did not allow him to play with long hair and a bearded face. Afonsinho's fight not only unlocked the gates for other so-called rebellious players, but also questioned the inflexible professional agreements that footballers were submitted to, and the ties that secured the players to their clubs even when their contracts had finished.

More recently, in 2010, students and scholars from Universidade Federal Fluminense in Rio de Janeiro, led by history professor Marcos Alvito, formed the National Association of Football Supporters (ANT). Targeting the protection of traditional football culture within the stadiums, in its foundational statement, ANT made strong demands in order to safeguard and promote supporters' rights.

ANT claimed that each stadium in the nation should retain a popular sector where fans could stand and cheer while paying low-cost ticket prices. They also sought enhanced public transport on game days; the end of tainted, anti-democratic and inept practices among clubs and federations board members. They also fought for the protection of human rights, namely the right of housing for vulnerable communities facing displacement due to the forthcoming mega sports events in Brazil.

However, the social movement within Brazilian football that so far had the most influence, not only in the sporting realm but also in broader society, was the *Bom Senso Futebol Clube* (BSFC). Born at the beginning of 2013, the BSFC was a new football political movement which was shaped by top footballers, many of whom went back to Brazil to end their playing days at home after a fruitful career in Europe or Asia.

These football stars put together this association so they could fight for a better football for players, for sponsors, for supporters, for broadcasters and for referees. After contrasting the respectable working situations they had abroad with the poor working milieu and unscrupulous practices from clubs' management that they saw in Brazil, they took their global knowledge in order to accomplish a better football community for everybody.

Players' unions have historically been weak in Brazil, and have never intensely supported players' rights nor fought against players' exploitation by clubs' managers and owners. The BSFC was born to seal this gap. Due to the high status of its frontrunners, it also attained significant support from media and prominent sport journalists.

The BSFC fast stretched its views through social media networks, obtaining support from hundreds of thousands of football fans all over the country. Highest on the BSFC's agenda was to guarantee the future sustainability of the sport. Central points in this agenda were that the national football calendar must be attuned in order to offer work prospects for minor clubs' players, so they can have a pay during the entire year and not only during the duration of the regional seasons.

An important issue targeted by the BSFC was the liability of club officials. The boards of Brazilian football clubs are not professional. They are elected to lead the club for a few years and the club's president and their board would never be liable for any wrongdoing during their term.

It was not uncommon for a club president to start in the role with high-debts with players and governments from the previous administration, but without any financial responsibility. The BSFC wanted to change this practice by making clubs' officials liable for their debts. BSFC wanted a bill that forced a professional club only be capable to spend what they collect.

The BSFC also fought for better conditions for supporters and to transform stadiums into a safe and comfortable leisure choice for families and fans.

The BSFC also led a considerable and so far unmatched political protest amongst A-level players through the 2013 Brazilian championship. As Jose Maria Marin, then the CBF's president refused to meet BSFC leaders to talk about their plans, and as various clubs continued their practice of delaying players' salaries, the BSFC ordered numerous protests across the country.

In a well-orchestrated way, and always prior to nationally broadcast games, supporters on the stands and players on the field raised banners in protest. In addition, players also sat on the pitches and declined to play for a few minutes at the start of the match.

As the CBF ordered the referees to penalize players for these actions by using yellow and red cards, the players started with a new protest tactic. During the first five minutes of each match, players from both teams would just pass the ball to each other without running or really engaging in the match, while being cheered by fans who supported the protests. BSFC also threatened CBF with an unparalleled players' strike, which would have serious international ramifications on the eve of 2014 World Cup.

The strike never occurred, and the BSFC has since changed its tactics by starting a significant political lobby with the Federal government and the national Parliament to approve a bill to reform Brazilian football. The proposed bill aimed to extinguish corrupt practices amongst clubs, support minor professional leagues as well as women's football, and make club directors accountable for clubs' financing difficulties.

The BSFC is a good example of robust, social organization that is currently happening across all levels of Brazilian society. As professional players, through BSFC, engage in social change, they joined the general society's efforts to build a new political order.

The social turbulence created by a diversity of social movements is revealing the stereotype of Brazilian people as passive and 'fiesta' people as wrong. It is a stereotype that has been masking the social reality of the country for decades.

8.

What the hell was the Maracanazo?

Throughout football history, World Cup finals matches have produced a number of epic episodes that have lasted in the social imagery for decades. Some final games are memorable due to sporting reasons, such as Brazil's 1970 final against Italy, a performance that remains alive in the lovers of the beautiful game.

Other finals though, are unforgettable due to their endless controversies, like the 1966 England victory over Germany, who has never ceased to protest against Hurst's second goal in extra time. For Germany, the ball did not cross the goal line.

There are even wins that were deemed so impossible that they became known as 'miracles', as the 1954 'Miracle of Bern' demonstrated. This was when Germany beat Puskás' Hungary under heavy rain after conceding the first two goals and despite having lost to the same team in the first round of the tournament, 8-3.

However, for Brazilians who became used to watching their Seleção playing in World Cup finals, there is a particular epic match that they want to forget, but the football world does not give them the chance to. This match occurred more than 70 years ago, on July 16th 1950. It was just the fourth World Cup, but every four years a new interpretation of this tale surfaces, with comments and arguments that intend to haunt Brazilians for that failure. The question that cannot be silenced is: do Brazilians really care about the Maracanazo 'tragedy'?

The 1950 defeat to Uruguay inside the Maracanã stadium was a tough one. Nearly 200,000 people, breaking every audience record for a football match, were there to celebrate the Seleção on that match day.

The popular appeal of both the final game and the national team was colossal.

During the preceding decades the modernisation of Brazilian society was accelerated: a mostly rural country was fast becoming an urban society. Football was a key part of this urbanisation process and had become intrinsically connected to Brazilian identity.

The game was quickly becoming one of the most popular leisure activities for all Brazilians. The sport was escaping the control of the country's social and cultural elites who wanted to keep its amateur profile. In 1933, it became fully professional.

After more than 300 years of African slavery, which left profound wounds across Brazilian society, former slaves and their offspring, with neither education nor professional preparation, saw the game as a sole chance of social ascent. A connection between football, race and social inclusion started to become clearer in the country.

During the 1930s, major political modifications unfolded in the country, with the end of the Old Republic and the start of the Second Republic. The new 1934 Constitution announced workers' rights and social security. Politicians deliberately used football's popular appeal to encourage a sense of national distinctiveness and to include the broader population in the building of the nation.

In 1940, from within a jam-packed football stadium, President Getulio Vargas signed into law the institution of a minimum salary for the first time in Brazilian history. This emblematic and potent act was a corroboration of the political drive of the modernising forces in the nation to link football to the progression of Brazilian citizenship.

The Brazilian intelligentsia likewise started to look at the game as the pre-eminent locus for the advertising of the supposed Brazilian 'racial democracy'. This concept, coined by famous Brazilian sociologist,

Gylberto Freyre, claimed that the country's racial blend of black and whites was exceptional. The Brazilian 'racial democracy', according to Freyre, was making a novel, inclusive, ethnically democratic civilization (a nation of mulattos), as it fitted the countrywide modernisation struggles throughout that era.

The 'country's democratic racial mix' archetype was rapidly attached to the Brazilian football flair as a unique and superior national appeal: the 'football-mulatto'. The Brazilian football playing style was a type of poetry, greater and contrasting to the European mechanical footballing style. Race and social class intertwined with football through the game's history in Brazil.

Prominent sports newspapers and reporters supported the game through their written pieces and radio shows. They participated in public events and debates to sell the game to different communities. The leading journalist of those times was Mario Filho, who in the previous years dynamically fought for the professionalisation of the game. Mario Filho used every single opportunity to advocate football as the major component of a national plan of social cohesion through sport.

Filho led the crusade to build the Maracanã stadium to host the 1950 World Cup, and the ground was renamed after him when he died in 1966.

Hence, in 1950 football already played a central role in a society that was quickly being transformed. Citizens of the new cities observed and participated in novel forms of leisure and the World Cup was an exceptional opportunity to consolidate all these changes. Moreover, it was a unique occasion to celebrate a new national identity by having football as its centrepiece.

Curiously, the 1950 World Cup was not played in the system we are currently used to seeing, that is, group phases and then an elimination system until the final match, where winners advance to the next round and losers go back home. For the 1950 tournament, the four teams that reached the final round (Brazil, Spain, Sweden and Uruguay) played in a single round-robin tournament and the champion would be the team with more points after all these games.

After two of these matches, Uruguay struggled to beat Sweden (3-2) and drew with Spain (2-2), accumulating three points (in those times a win was worth only two points). On the other hand, Brazil was cruising through the round-robin, showing a beautiful and offensive playing style, with four points after demolishing Sweden (7-1) and Spain (6-1). The euphoria in the country was high, as a draw against Uruguay in the final match would see the *Seleção* win its first World Cup title.

Journalists, including Mario Filho, football managers, politicians and the general public were already celebrating. The atmosphere in Rio de Janeiro was as if the *Seleção* was already the world champion. On the morning of the final match, Rio's streets were crowded, and there was a party atmosphere in the air.

Prior to the match, Rio's mayor delivered a speech inside the packed Maracanã stadium, where he told the crowd that "You Brazilians, who in just a few hours will be crowned World Champions!". There was just one small, overlooked detail: within this entire festive atmosphere, Brazilians forgot to think that they still had to draw with or beat the last opponent before lifting the trophy.

Unfortunately for the whole country, *La Celeste* (The Sky Blue as the Uruguayan team is known) had other plans. Their coach was actually conservative and in his pre-game talk instructed the team to play in a defensive style otherwise, according to him, they would be smashed by the *Seleção*.

As soon as he left the change room though, *La Celeste's* captain Obdulio Varella talked to his team in a different way. Contrary to their coach's strategies, he argued to his teammates that playing defensively would just give more space to the *Seleção's* offensive style and this would fire up the stands. In a touching speech, he appealed to his players for them to face the adversity together and not be intimidated by the Brazilian crowd. He finished his talk with a sentence that would resonate for several years in South America: "The ones on the stands do not play".

Varella was pivotal to the Uruguayan team's win. His bravery orchestrated the Maracanazo. Led by Varella, La Celeste could contain all the *Seleção* advances during the first half. Early in the second half of the match, Friaça scored for the *Seleção*, and the crowd went crazy.

Without being intimidated and in order to calm down the atmosphere, Varella argued with the referee about an alleged off side in the *Seleção's* goal for several minutes. The goal was confirmed, but Varella's intent was successful. He carried the ball to the centre line and screamed to his team: "A*hora vamos a ganar* !"(Now let's win this match!).

And they did.

La Celeste started to explore the *Seleção's* defensive gaps. After 20 minutes, Schiaffino equalised for Uruguay.

The crowd was subdued, but not yet alarmed as Brazil would still be champions with a draw.

However, a tireless Varella was running around the field asking for '*mas alma, mas alma'* (more soul, more soul!) from his teammates. The crowd became tense and not as vocal as it was before Uruguay's goal. Varella's voice could be heard across the field.

Then, in the 79th minute, the impossible happened: Ghiggia ran on the right wing of the Brazilian box and hassled by the Brazilian defender, it looked as if he would cross the ball, but instead he shot for goal. The ball travelled between the near post and the hands of Barbosa, the *Seleção's* goal keeper.

No sound could be heard in the last minutes of the game.

The match finished and the unimaginable tragedy had just happened: *La Celeste* beat the *Seleção* inside *Maracanã*.

The silence was deafening. Two hundred thousand people left the stadium without a word and without belief that they lost a title that was taken for granted. Jules Rimet, then FIFA's president, had planned to deliver a speech in Portuguese while presenting the trophies to the teams. However, nobody showed up for the presentation ceremony and Rimet was left alone on the field and had to call Varella to deliver the trophy.

The 22 gold medals with the *Seleção's* players' names engraved on them earlier coined by the National Sports Council (CBD) were not presented either. Later that night, several hours after the end of the game, there were thousands of people still wandering around the city, in a state of astonishment.

Nevertheless, the Maracanazo shock was quickly revenged as the *Seleção* and Brazilian clubs ruled the international football scene in the coming years.

The *Seleção* won three out of four World Cups between 1958 and 1970. Pelé turned into the greatest player in the football realm, recording more than 1,000 goals as both a professional and non-professional player by 1969. Pelé's club, Santos FC, gained two successive Libertadores Cup and World Club titles (1962 and 1963). Maracanã was regularly occupied by large audiences. During those years, Brazilian football was living its 'golden era'.

The Maracanazo was definitely a miserable moment for the nation, but it did not last too long as the overall success of Brazilian football made people forget that failure. Brazilians were happy with the national sport for years.

There was just one person who never forgot the Maracanazo. We could even say that he was the only perpetual victim of this tale.

His name is Barbosa, the *Seleção*'s goal keeper. He was never 'acquitted' by the press and in the minds of the public because of that second goal. Many years ago he declared that the maximum imprisonment time by Brazilian laws was 30 years, but he was still serving his 'sentence' after 50 years since his 'crime'.

In 1993, when he was 72 years old, Barbosa went to visit the *Seleção*'s camp as they prepared for a crucial match against Uruguay in the 1994 World Cup qualifiers. However, he was denied entry into the team's headquarters and not allowed to speak to the players. Parreira, then the *Seleção*'s coach, did not want any "negative vibrations from the past" influencing his team.

Barbosa passed away at 79 and right until his death he was often called by different media sectors to explain that fatidical goal. Films were made and books and dissertations were written about Barbosa. Some argued that racism played a central role in the goalkeeper's unhappy saga.

Barbosa was an outstanding black athlete who endured in silence all the accusations of being responsible for the 1950 defeat. Gylberto Freyre's 'Brazilian racial democracy' is yet to enter the goalkeeper's area.

The only 'Maracanazo' that still curses Brazil is the persistent racism against black people across the whole country.

9.

June 2013: A social revolution in the mid of international football?

Twenty cents of a Brazilian Real, or just seven cents of an American dollar. That was the announced increase in public transport fares by the authorities in São Paulo city, the largest South American metropolis. The increase was broadcast in June 2013, not long before the start of the FIFA Confederations Cup. It ignited an explosion of street demonstrations and police savagery in Paulista Avenue, the iconic heart of São Paulo's business and economic power.

The marches against the twenty cent fare raise were initially called by the *Movimento Passe Livre* (MPL, the 'Free Fare Movement'). The MPL is a social movement whose main platform is to fight for better and free public transport across Brazilian cities.

Since 2005, the MPL has launched an agenda recognizing that working class people who live in the peripheral zones of Brazilian metropolitan areas spend too many hours in, and pay too much for, low quality public transport. The MPL has also consulted with academic and public authorities to back up their demands for free public transport as a social right for workers within urban settings.

The MPL has affiliated sections in southern and northern Brazilian cities (such as Florianópolis and Salvador respectively) where they had already led enormous protests against the poor public transport conditions. These demonstrations were also strongly repressed by local police.

However, it was the demonstrations in the heart of the highly visible Paulista Avenue in São Paulo city that became a moment that changed the country, right on the verge of the 2013 FIFA Confederations Cup.

The facts: in early June 2013, São Paulo's mayor announced the twenty cent raise on bus fares (aligned with the same raise imposed by state government to metro fares). The MPL quickly responded that the rise was unjustifiable and would add an extra burden to the peripheral youth and working class. The MPL presented studies showing that populations living in fringe urban areas were either walking hundreds of extra kilometres a year to go to work or their study places, or just stayed home as they could not afford the fares.

Subsequently, the MPL called for demonstrations in the Paulista Avenue on weekdays. They blocked the traffic during peak hours and created urban chaos as they were met by police repression. Next, the Folha de São Paulo (The 'São Paulo Herald', a major Brazilian newspaper based in São Paulo) launched an editorial demanding that the authorities "take back Paulista Avenue" from the demonstrators. This was the sign that the state government was waiting for.

As the MPL called for new marches, the police met them with extreme violence. Riot police trapped the marchers on their way to the demonstration and then threw gas bombs and rubber bullets towards them, while battering the ones who tried to escape. Among the thousands of injured demonstrators, a Folha de São Paulo reporter lost an eye due to a rubber bullet.

If this level of police violence was not uncommon in the outskirts of the cities, it was magnified as it happened in the Paulista Avenue and surrounding areas, a central place for business and leisure where people expect to be able to walk around safely. Even the Folha de São Paulo, faced by the images and consequences of the extreme police violence, retreated from its original idea and asked that city and state authorities call the MPL for a round of negotiations.

Subsequent to the Paulista Avenue bloody battles, the key actors reshaped their tactics. The MPL regrouped to plan their strategic new steps to face this unprecedented level of state violence. São Paulo's mayor, from the 'left-oriented' workers party (PT), after some reluctance, indicated he was willing to open negotiations with the MPL and even cancel the fare raise

In the meantime, the social landscape was pointing to an important change in the scope of the demonstrations.

Motivated by the powerful images of the street marchers for better public transport, a commanding message started to circulate initially within social media. Rapidly, this message then gained momentum on the streets: "It's not only for the twenty cents". Its meaning was clear; Brazilian people should fight for much more than the twenty cents public transport increase, they should fight for "everything that is wrong in the country".

Suddenly, demonstrations were organised to protest for better education and health systems, and against other public grievances. The MPL quickly responded by stating that their agenda was focused on the public transport's price increase. They insisted that their fight was for cancellation of the twenty cent rise, with the long term goal still being the demand for free public transport.

Consequently the MPL did not show any support for the new demonstrations. They declared that these rallies did not have any dedicated plan but rather just provided generic slogans against 'the whole thing'.

The MPL was out but the willingness to march against the system was there. Along with the street marches in the major Brazilian cities, June 2013 saw many young people occupy the national parliament buildings in the Federal capital of Brasilia. As many cities postponed the increase in the bus fares, the protesters kept advancing on the streets.

The momentum could not have been better. With the 2013 Confederations Cup approaching, the world's eyes were turning to Brazil. FIFA, the other national teams and the international media were arriving in the country. It was an ideal moment to protest and to demand 'schools and hospitals with FIFA standards', the same luxurious requirements that FIFA sought with World Cup stadiums.

As the protesters occupied the streets and FIFA officials could not leave their hotels, there were rumours that FIFA had a 'plan B' and would transfer the competition to another country.

As Sepp Blatter, then FIFA president left the country, the talks intensified that FIFA would relocate the 2014 World Cup to a safer place. Several hands around the globe went up to signal their willingness to host the event in the case of relocation.

As we know, this did not happen. At the end of the tournament and as the streets were calming down, Blatter returned to the country. Brazil managed not only to successfully host the Confederations Cup, but also to win it, leveraging the hopes that the 2014 World Cup would be as successful as the Confederations Cup. The win also gave Brazilian supporters the expectations that the *Seleção* could win its sixth World Cup in the following year.

The 'June 2013 revolution' in Brazil brought several unexpected social and political consequences to the country. It is clear that public turbulence was nothing original in Brazil: what was new was the world spotting it through the magnifying lenses provided by the international football events that the country was hosting.

June 2013 was a turning point. For many it was seen as a social revolution, or as evidence that the Brazilian population would have the means to challenge for better social rights. However, it can also be interpreted as a major coup for the conservative forces that did not want to see further growth of social rights in the country, nor Brazil's global political and economic expansion. For the first time in decades, the right wing groups realised that they could use the power of the streets to push their own conservative agenda in the national political scenario.

The momentum of international sports events was a perfect opportunity to launch an offensive against the 'progressive' government and its so-called agenda of social justice. After all, the government that promoted a limited social inclusion for the millions of disenfranchised Brazilians, who for centuries lived in misery and without social rights, was the same government that used the World Cup and the Olympics to grow Brazil's international projection and global influence.

The right-wing was surfing over Brazilians' will to march against the corruption symbolised by FIFA's events in the country to promote their own agenda contrary to the minimal advancement of social justice in the country.

Some who joined the June 2013 demonstrations described them as fervently exciting occasions full of music and dancing, in a typical Brazilian Carnavale style. However, more experienced observers could see how the demonstrations quickly escalated into tense, alarming encounters packed with provocateurs and undercover militaries concealed by 'Anonymous' façades. It was the right-wing testing the powerful tool of street protests. It would not take long for the conservative forces to take the steps to demand the impeachment of an elected president.

As the varying narratives over the June 2013 protests are still in dispute, the undeniable fact is that those demonstrations changed the political and social landscape of the country forever.

Unfortunately, from the most blinded loyal supporter of the *Seleção*, to the biggest critic of the team and the World Cup hosting in general, nobody would have imagined how a country could deteriorate in such a short timeframe – from a major player in the international arena with expanded social rights to its marginalised people, to a country where the social conditions are moving backwards to the ones similar to the early 20th century.

These are much worse consequences than losing 7-1 to Germany in a World Cup semi-final at home.

10.

The World Cup trophy is ours?
Bye-bye to the football nation

"The World Cup trophy is ours/no one can match a Brazilian". These were the initial verses of a *'marchinha'*, a song in Carnaval rhythm created by Wagner Maugeri, Lauro Müller, Maugeri Sobrinho and Victor Dagô to celebrate the first *Seleção* victory in a World Cup. The year was 1958 and Garrincha and Pelé had just mesmerised the world in Sweden, beating the host team 5-2 in the final.

It was not long before that conquest that the 'football-land myth' was not only spread, but also consolidated around the country and the world. The Brazilian football-samba style, the *'jogo bonito'*, was one of the most important features of Brazilian identity that the world would recognise and praise in the years to come.

The 'football-land' myth was invigorated in the following decade because of the continuing success of Brazilian football on the international stage. After the 1958 win, the *Seleção* added two World Cup trophies to its cabinet by securing the 1962 and the 1970 tournaments, playing in the same, memorable style and conquering hearts and minds across the globe.

This was the most extreme proficuous period of Brazilian football history, particularly when football genuinely brought joy to Brazilians. The myth of the 'football-land' was well solidified and had become a central component of Brazil's social life and identity, perhaps the only national symbol of which Brazilians could be proud of.

However, as much as football was embedded in Brazil's soul, things changed. Since the 1950s and in the following decades, the country went through a huge urbanisation process, which brought cultural diversity to its cities but also plenty of social issues such as the advancement of *favelas* and other chaotic urban dwellings. The country also went through a homicidal dictatorship, in which the scars are yet to heal, even more than two decades after its end. The 1979 Amnesty Law brought back the political exiles but never allowed the destiny of hundreds of 'political disappearances' to be revealed.

Hence, given all these social and political factors, plus a continuing 'crisis' of Brazilian football, and despite persevering in the social imagination as a strong tale, the 'football-land' myth has been clearly under risk in the country since the mid-1970s.

Although Brazil won the World Cup in 1994 and 2002, previous and ongoing years of crooked practices allowed this myth to decline. Actually, what myth could survive with decreasing TV audiences and crowd attendance, a worsening of working conditions for the majority of professional players, and the lack of a rational schedule for national competitions? Furthermore, the economic failures of Brazil's main clubs, corrupt refereeing, violence in stadiums, and a non-stop departure of the country's best players to ply their trade abroad?

References in the media to Brazil as the 'football-land' have been in decline since the beginning of the twenty-first century.

The decay of the 'football-land' myth seemed to be complete by 2014, especially when people went public on social media to demonstrate their dislike to the 'CBF's team'. To stop calling the *Seleção* by its cheerful nickname and linking the team to the corrupt sporting body that 'owns' it, indicated the extension of the damage inflicted in the symbolic dimension between the 'football-land' icon and its people.

These sorts of messages have been around since earlier this century. Due to their powerful political and legal network, Teixeira and the CBF could escape nearly unharmed from the two Parliamentary inquiries that revealed their corrupt practices in the beginning of the 2000s.

However, the 'football-land' myth did not have the same destiny. National representatives who were part of the inquiries and were not in Teixeira's pocket, after struggling without success to move the inquiries' results to the courts, declared their absolute repugnance for all things football related.

Their pungent testimonies at the end of the inquiries summarised a feeling of repulsion towards the myth. In a surprising move, they even advised Brazilian people to stop putting their hard-earned cash and their emotional energies into anything related to football. These representatives gave up supporting their teams and even their once beloved *Seleção*.

This was another blow to the 'football-land' myth, which was complemented by influential sports journalists putting pressure on the *Seleção*'s players to act against Teixeira and his practices. These journalists, who once treated the *Seleção* as the most important national symbol, could not separate the team and the CBF management anymore. It was with reason: Teixeira's rule demonstrated to be extremely lucrative for the CBF – and also him – but not as productive for Brazilian football as a whole.

While the CBF's finances improved, its investment in football declined. During Teixeira's years, 60 per cent of CBF spending was on its own management, with merely 27 per cent being spent on football programs. This lack of funds caused, as already pointed to, the degeneration in playing and working conditions at the professional tiers, resulting in a significant exodus of Brazilian players to overseas clubs.

Adding to the weaknesses of the Brazilian teams were the bad stadium conditions, violence between supporters, a calendar that privileged the main CBF broadcast partner and not the public, amongst other management issues. It is not hard to understand why the 'football-land' myth was in accelerated decline in the previous decades.

All these problems operated to cause slow but persistent erosion in the football milieu in Brazil, landing numerous blows on the footballing national identity. They weakened the sentimental bonds that linked the Brazilian public with the sport and its main icon, the *Seleção*.

The decrease of football's symbolic element does not mean that football will not continue to be important for Brazilians. Despite all these social changes, in spite of the CBF's lacklustre management and even taking into account the diversity of sports practised nowadays by Brazilians, football still remains the number one sport in the country, both in terms of leisure activity, as well as a strong institution and competitive sport.

However, prior and during the 2014 World Cup, Brazilians were not deceived anymore by another World Cup trophy. They have grown up and were worried about achieving a trophy that they have never earned before — social justice for all in the country.

PART 2:
Living the World Cup

11.

The magic in the air: was the World Cup a megalomaniac project' that went well?

FIFA and the Brazilian government had just one bet: football's magical nature.

The negative international and national press coverage in the months before the World Cup was surmounting. There were predictions of unfinished stadiums and airports' ongoing construction offering unsafe and dangerous prospects for tourists. Moreover, the entire world was watching enormous street demonstrations and public dissatisfaction with the way the tournament was being put together.

Nevertheless, the World Cup organisers stood still. According to them, as soon as the ball started to roll, everybody would just join in the football party.

They were proven correct. When the games started, the football magic entered the air. On the field, there was a largely optimistic narrative that the football quality displayed in most of the matches was fantastic. Juca Kfouri, a major Brazilian sport journalist who initially opposed Brazil's World Cup's bid reported that:

... so far, this is an exceptional World Cup, with the highest goals per game average since the 1970 World Cup.

According to many Brazilians, there was a key, outstanding reason for the exceptional level of football played during this tournament: the Brazilian mystique. My Brazilian friends, who once were angry with the World Cup preparations, reconsidered their thoughts as soon as the tournament started by going on social media to declare that:

... a country's love for the World Cup and the streets' atmosphere is what matters;what's the point of having everything well put and on time if nobody parties like us?

Juca Kfouri added to their comments by saying that:

... there is a breeze of Garrincha's spirit and futebol-arte blowing in every game.

The main narrative that filled the major social and mainstream media channels as soon as the World Cup kicked-off was that the 'gringos' had never seen "something like that, and just loved it". The warm cheering that underdog sides – such as Australia, Iran or Bosnia-Herzegovina – received from the audience also helped in building up the excellent atmosphere in Brazilian stadiums.

This 'football wishful thinking' is not new for Brazilians. In the 2006 World Cup, for instance, the *Seleção* had a bad and messy preparation for the tournament. The team leaders – stars such as Ronaldo and Roberto Carlos – were visibly out of shape. On top of that, the team's key players were more likely to be partying during the competition than concentrating on the matches.

However, nothing affected the faith in the *Seleção*. Neither the lack of training nor fitness, nor the players' agitated night life would be enough to defeat us. "We thought we would somehow score at any moment in that match" declared Cafu, the team's captain, after a defeat against France caused the *Seleção*'s early elimination from the tournament.

It wasn't preparation, an innovative tactical move or a substitution, but somehow, with a magic trick, the *Seleção* would score and beat their opponents. That's how Brazilians used to live. During the 2014 World Cup serious media analysts claimed that the World Cup should always be played on the South American subcontinent – "there is no bigger passion than ours" they asserted.

This passion was infectious. The players felt it, and that pushed the World Cup matches to another level.

This 'wishful thinking' played a considerable role in Brazil's World Cup planning. In 2007, when Brazil 'won' without opposition the hosting rights to the 2014 tournament, the international and the national economic atmosphere were different and more positive for Brazil.

Lula, Brazil's first working-class elected president in 2002 and re-elected in 2006, had big plans for the country. He wanted to make up for so much lost time. After decades of recession and lack of public investment, Brazilians were seeing a new era of growth and government venture. With a growing economy that placed Brazil amongst the larger countries in the world and the global acceptance of its social inclusion programs and its positive benefits, Brazil aimed to be at the centre of the world.

As a result, Brazil would certainly organise the best World Cup ever. Lula, a football lover, regarded the World Cup as an opportunity to promote Brazil on the global stage – and, of course, to leverage his political party for more years in power.

The plans were ambitious – a few would categorise them as megalomaniacal.

Of course, they involved Brazil's complicated political scenario. With 27 states governed by different political forces – and all of them eager for a piece of the World Cup's pie – Brazil was not happy to have only eight hosting cities, as FIFA considered adequate.

After lengthy political negotiations, the local organisers and the state and federal governments decided to build 12 stadiums. Some of these stadiums were built in places such as Manaus, Brasilia or Cuiaba where, unfortunately, there has never been professional football to justify these new constructions.

The stakes were high. Brazil rapidly became a huge construction site. Airports were revamped, 'urban mobility' renovations spread across the country and stadiums built – there were visible signs of a new era after decades of lack of public investment. The grandiosity of the project faced not only certain corruption allegations, but also the changing political and economic scenario and the social convulsions that it caused.

Education levels were a key factor that were not considered in Brazil's World Cup preparation: despite being one of the world's top seven economies, Brazil had shameful levels of social inequality.

Educational opportunities were still an issue for Brazil as the country prepared for the World Cup. The fact was that there were not enough human resources to evaluate and to run all the projects necessary for the World Cup.

In the years prior to the event, the federal government made huge investments and created several policies to attract lower class students to universities: University for All – PROUNI – was the most well-known of these policies. However, these educational investments would not produce tangible and sustainable outcomes in time for the World Cup.

In short, Brazil was not fully equipped to plan such an enormous event. There was still a lack of engineers working for the government banks that provide the loans to analyse major construction project applications. There was also a shortage of qualified people to ensure that the public resources invested would not be misused. Brazil's educational inequality needed to be further addressed to ensure that the social legacy of such a major event was consistent.

Regardless, Brazilian authorities were sure that the magic would work again, and Brazil somehow would organise a great event. A few constructions plans were abandoned and this sort of legacy was never to be what was, at first, promised.

But there was no thought of main plans changing, so the event could be hosted in existing renovated stadiums, therefore lessening the public expenditure – but still allowing Brazil to host a great World Cup.

The works proved to be successful. Brazil showed to itself and to the international community that it could organise a great World Cup, despite the dire predictions.

Flights and airports did not face many delays and were considered a tangible legacy for Brazil. The new stadiums looked great, regardless of a few break- ins and issues with food supply that happened during the competition. And, of course, the excellent football quality, due to the unbeatable Brazilian atmosphere, was vivid and reliable evidence that the football gods are, indeed, Brazilians.

Yet, a few demonstrators insisted on parading on World Cup streets while facing unprecedented police violence. Commentators said they lost the momentum and could not mobilise larger crowds as everyone wanted to party and enjoy the moment.

I would rather think that these protestors were a collective conscience that constantly asked us what happened to the 250,000 vulnerable Brazilians forced to relocate in the name of this giant party.

12.

Futebol-arte, the soul of the game: a tribute to Garrincha

Mané Garrincha (1933–1983) became known as the greatest dribbler of all time and is one the major icons of Brazilian football-art (*futebol-arte or 'jogo bonito'*). He never thought that his legs – he was sometimes known as the 'Angel with Bent Legs', with his right leg pointing inwards and his left leg pointing outwards – were a problem.

As Argentincan writer Jorge Luis Borges said, a man needs to accept that:

... whatever happens to him is an instrument given for an end – this is even stronger in the case of the artist.

Garrincha used his crooked legs as an inventive tool to take advantage of his opponents. Nobody could foresee which direction he was going to run with the ball. It was nearly impossible to stop Garrincha's dribbling.

Garrincha is an important symbol of futebol-arte. By winning two World Cups in a row (1958 in Sweden and 1962 in Chile) with Brazil's national team, he achieved outstanding international results. Importantly, Garrincha also left a real artistic impression on world football with his beautiful aesthetic playing style and constant improvisations.

Garrincha is the evidence that futebol-arte is more than simply a tactic. It is a destiny – a destiny of joy. Hence Garrincha also being known as the 'Joy of the People'.

There are famous anecdotes of the lead-up to the 1958 final. The *Seleção's* coach used a blackboard to identify the Sweden team, its moves, and what Brazil should do to beat them. Garrincha asked his coach if he had already agreed with the other team that they would be playing like this. It was a demonstration of Garrincha's understanding of the game as a field for improvisation rather than well-planned strategies.

Garrincha's question and style were the synthesis of football and art, the improvisation that produces unforgettable artistic football moments. Futebol-arte is beyond what was described by University of Sydney academic Steve Georgakis as "a battle between aesthetics and results". Futebol-arte is the soul of the football game – or at least of the version developed in South America.

The roots of the idea of futebol-arte can be found in Gilberto Freyre's concept of Brazilian 'racial democracy'. Freyre (1900-1987) was one of the leading sociologists in Brazil in the 20th century. The author of *Masters and Slaves*, Freyre considered whether people from different 'races' lived in harmony in Brazil.

Most importantly for Freyre, the mixing of the country's black and white people would create a different form of culture and civilisation, the 'mulattos'. Freyre's thoughts also spread towards football, and its importance in development of the national uniqueness.

According to Freyre, the 'football-mulatto' played in Brazil as a result of racial miscegenation was opposed to the game played by Europeans. Freyre believed that the style of football played in Brazil had its own rhythm, a result of the cultural mix under way in the country. Brazilian football was a sort of dance where the actual Brazil, the mulatto one, would scintillate. On the contrary, European football was excessively mechanical, with no room for creativity.

In summary, Freyre's theory argued that the European style was Apollonian and acknowledged hard work and collectivism. On the other hand, the Brazilian style was Dionysian, a celebration of individual spontaneity. Freyre's football-mulatto claimed that the Brazilian style was poetry, while the European style could be described as prose.

As the poet John B. Wain says:

... poetry is to prose as dancing is to walking.

Improvisation and individual spontaneity are the foundations of futebol-arte and can be found in different historical moments of the Brazilian team. The 1958 and the 1962 Brazilian teams were full of futebol-arte, and the 1970 *Seleção* was one of the finest teams in the futebol-arte's history.

But after that, Brazil went off track by trying to mimic the European Apollonian style. Brazil became dominated by the military, and that promoted an anti-democratic and autocratic atmosphere in the national football team. The creativity associated with futebol-arte cannot flourish in an authoritarian atmosphere as it needs liberty. It doesn't come from outside or from above it comes from within, it comes from the heart.

It was only under coach Tele Santana that Brazil recovered its famous futebol-arte style. Even if they didn't win a World Cup, Zico, Sócrates and their teammates in the 1982 team will always be revered by Brazilians as true representatives of futebol- arte. The pleasure and the art they put into everything they did was clear.

As with Garrincha, Sócrates had a physical issue: his feet were too small for his stature, so he couldn't turn his body as fast as he wanted. Yet instead of complaining, Sócrates developed a unique heel-kick which is one of the most acclaimed futebol-arte tricks ever.

Brazil hasn't produced an inspirational footballing generation like the 1982 one since. The 1994 team which won that year's World Cup was coached by Carlos Alberto Parreira. When asked why he played a defensive style that did not pay tribute to the Brazilian traditions,

Parreira declared that:

... magic and dreams are finished in football. We have to combine technique and efficiency.

Even if Brazilian players continue to shine on the international stage, we are still to see the true futebol-arte coming back.

The most recent style of play to capture global imagination is the Spanish 'tiki- taka', a highly successful model which emphasises possession of the ball and fast passing between three or more players until a defensive gap is found. Tiki-taka produced great successes and magnificent aesthetic footballing moments, yet it is anything but improvisation and poetry. Tiki-taka is a well-calculated tactical system repeated to exhaustion, which is exactly what Parreira described when he talked about magic and dreams being overrun by a new combination of skill and productivity.

Tiki-taka is unusual in that it does not represent the aesthetic side of football in opposition to the 'football of results'. It actually combines aesthetics with results in an incredibly well-trained machine with no room for improvisation. Tiki-taka is a beautiful machine, but it is still prose.

Futebol-arte goes further than this combination: it takes football to another level. Futebol-arte goes to the stands and to the world from the pitch. It is a way of life.

The best example of futebol-arte that was seen in the 2014 World Cup was the Netherlands' Robin van Persie's goal against Spain. Like a bird, he flew to be happy, with no fear, crafting real poetry in the air before heading the ball towards the net. Van Persie's goal was a tribute to Garrincha, a nickname that means 'little bird'.

Perhaps this is what futebol-arte would be confined to in the future: a few moments of pure imagination and poetry lost amongst the intense commodification of the game and the villainy of its owners. Futebol-arte needs freedom to flourish once more.

Yet there were some Brazilians still dreaming that the *Seleção* would take inspiration from past generations and once more revitalize futebol-arte. Their will was that the World Cup, and all the thoughts of social upheaval that it had catalysed and provoked, would be sufficient to redeem and liberate the game again. For them, the 'best World Cup ever' would revive futebol- arte and install a new order in the football world.

Unfortunately, this needed more actual action than wishful thinking.

13.

FIFA go home —
but first try an acarajé and pay a taxi fare

Francisco Vargas was a humble taxi driver in Vitória, the capital city of the Espirito Santo state in Brazil. For the past 40 years he worked at a taxi stand in front of the *Estádio da Desportiva* (The Desportiva Stadium) in the Cariacica neighbourhood. He made his living by driving an average of 16 customers per day.

However, because the Estádio da Desportiva was the Australian team's training base for the World Cup, Francisco's taxi stand was relocated to a street behind the *Estádio* before and during the World Cup. The *Estádio* was then declared a 'FIFA zone', and nothing or nobody could be in its way. A FIFA employee replaced the taxi stands signs by a sign of 'no parking or stopping anytime'.

The damage was immediate: Francisco lost 40% of his daily customers.

This was the type of minor intervention in daily life that made Brazilians angry at FIFA – and with the Brazilian government, because it approved the World Cup General Statute, a bill that allowed FIFA to modify Brazilian laws and cultural traditions, making minor but also major alterations in Brazilians' lives before and during the event.

One example of these changes was the reintroduction of the sale of beer and alcoholic drinks in Brazilian stadiums. Alcohol has been banned from the country's stadiums since 2003. This ban came after years of academic research and activist struggle. The government, the judiciary and researchers such as Dr Heloisa Reis from Universidade Estadual de Campinas understood that limiting alcohol sales during professional matches would aid the difficult task of tackling stadium violence in Brazil.

Nevertheless, in a total act of disrespect for Brazil's laws and social context, alcohol came back to the arenas for the World Cup. FIFA, which has as one of its major sponsors a Belgian-US brewing company, pushed the Brazilian government hard.

In 2012, the Brazilian President signed a law that allowed alcohol back in to World Cup stadiums because FIFA considers alcohol to be 'part of the World Cup culture'. It will be interesting to see how the conflict between local culture and traditions versus 'the World Cup culture' (meaning sponsorship deals) will play out during the 2022 Qatar World Cup.

FIFA demands respect for what it sees as 'football culture' but showed disrespect for a country's dearest cultural symbols and traditions. The history of the *acarajé* and the *Baianas* in Salvador is a good illustration. However, this time, the Brazilian people won, and FIFA had to adjust its requirements in order to 'swallow' this traditional food embedded in the culture of the Bahia state and football customs.

Acarajé is a dish made from peeled black-eyed peas formed into a ball and then deep-fried in dendê palm oil. It is a hot spicy snack that is found anywhere in the streets of Salvador, the capital city of Bahia, in Brazil's northeast.

The Baianas (Bahia native women, mostly descendent from African slaves) dress in their typical all-white *candomblé* dresses, sit in their small kiosks on Salvador's streets, and make and sell acarajé on the spot – charging around USD$2 each.

Baianas used to make and sell acarajé in the Fonte Nova Stadium in Salvador – they have done so since its opening in 1951. It is a tradition passed from mother to daughter through generations of families who make a living by selling this street food. If you go to a Brazilian city and walk its streets, you'll quickly notice how many Brazilians earn a living selling food and other goods on the streets. It is an important part of the local economy that can't be simply ignored.

However, during any World Cup, FIFA becomes the owner of the stadiums and their surroundings. There is a protected 'FIFA zone' that goes two kilometres around the venues. Inside these 'occupied zones', FIFA only allows its sponsors merchandise to be displayed and sold.

No local food if you're from overseas, and travelled to lovely Salvador with its streets full of colonial history to watch Netherlands beat Spain. Instead of tasting the delicious acarajé, FIFA dictated that you could only eat a Big Mac or a Happy Meal.

However, FIFA would never have expected the reaction of the Baianas.

When the Fonte Nova stadium was about to reopen after being renovated for the 2013 Confederations Cup, Rita Maria dos Santos, the president of the Association of Baianas Acarajé and Porridge vendors (ABAM) heard that FIFA wouldn't allow them to work inside or close to the new stadium.

Rita quickly started to email the authorities until she was contacted by the online activist organisation, Change.org.

Working with the organisation, she put together an online petition which quickly garnered international attention.

With 17,000 signatures, Rita pushed the Brazilian government to help their cause.

Dilma Rousseff, the then Brazilian president, was personally involved with the acarajé issue. FIFA had to step back. Even with restrictions imposed by the FIFA standards – such as not using nail polish ("is McDonald's under the same restrictions?" Rita ironically asked) – Baianas were allowed to sell their delicious acarajés in the Arena Fonte Nova.

Stadium names were another hard question for Brazilians to cope with. Brazilians have been calling their football stadiums 'Estádios' since they were built, 'Estádios' being the Portuguese word for stadiums. FIFA not only called them 'arenas', but also wanted people to refer to them in a standardised way.

The most notorious case was the stadium in Brasilia, the 'Estádio Nacional de Brasilia Mané Garrincha', named after the icon of Brazilian football-arte. Twice world champion with the Seleção (in 1958 and 1962), Garrincha's memory lives on in the heart of Brazilians (he died in 1983). He was the best player in the 1962 campaign after Pelé was injured. Garrincha, with his amazing dribbling skills, represents the purest tradition of Brazilian football.

However, the local football federation, controlled by conservative 'big-wigs', did not want Garrincha's name associated with the stadium. It was only after a long battle, which involved civil society pressure and the national Parliament passing a bill, that this new stadium could be named after Garrincha.

Even so, FIFA did not want people calling the new 'arena' as 'Mané Garrincha' during the events it organised. FIFA wanted all stadiums following their proscribed standard. It wanted the stadium simply called Estádio Nacional de Brasilia. Even so, people did not care. Everyone called it 'Mané Garrincha'.

The list of FIFA 'invasions' go on. FIFA's profit for the Brazil World Cup reached US$2 billion – 66% more than the 2010 World Cup in South Africa. FIFA, its workers and partners did not pay any tax while working in Brazil, which is the norm with a FIFA event.

Brazilians would pay the full bill, however, and were not happy with that. A few, such as the Baianas led by Rita dos Santos (who is also the mother of Felipe, a former Flamengo goalkeeper) organised peaceful but firm protest actions against these cultural and economic invasions.

Others went to the streets, and displayed angry slogans and chanted against FIFA, as well as the federal and state governments.

However, demonstrators faced unparalleled violence and repression from the police and the security forces during the World Cup. Their basic human rights were disrespected every single day while the tournament went on.

Others, such as Francisco Vargas, the taxi driver from Vitoria, acted differently. Aware that FIFA would not pay his monthly bills, he returned to his former taxi stand. If someone said that parking there was forbidden and tried to book him, he would play dumb, pretending he hadn't understood what was going on. It looked like he had already learnt a few cultural lessons from the Australians of resisting authority who were controlling his city.

14.

Brazil and Argentina: a friendly rivalry

Argentineans invaded Brazil during the World Cup. While Brazilians had plenty of political, economic and social issues to deal with as a consequence of the tournament, their South American rivals were just happy to go to Brazil and celebrate their team and football culture in Brazilian cities.

Hundreds of thousands of Argentineans crossed Brazilian southern borders, even without money to buy a ticket for a match or to pay for accommodation. They wanted to be part of the party, and they could sleep on Rio de Janeiro's beaches.

Argentina making it to the World Cup final at the Maracanã, after Germany's crushing defeat of Brazil's *Seleção*, also added a nice flavour to the Argentinean invasion, and boosted their well-known arrogance. Their chants on the Rio de Janeiro and São Paulo streets provocatively noted how they felt superior over their traditional local rivals.

The Brazil and Argentina rivalry goes beyond the football pitch. The quest for political and cultural supremacy in South America has a long history that starts in the colonial times. In the time of the great maritime European explorers, Portugal and Spain split the South American continent between them. But the fighting for pieces of land continued for centuries

For instance, Uruguay has been one of the most contested spaces in South America. It was claimed by both Spanish and Portuguese empires before becoming independent as a result of the *Cisplatina* war at the beginning of the 19th century. This was an armed conflict between the Portuguese empire (Brazil, Portugal and Algarves) and the United Provinces of the Plata River – led by Argentina. In Argentinean historiography, this war is known as 'war against the Brazilian Empire'.

After that, and in the past 200 years, the relationship between Argentina and Brazil has seen many changes in accordance with each country's aspirations of regional leadership and their connections with global powers such as England and the US. Generically, we may say that if the 19th century was marked by a great rivalry between the countries, the first half of the 20th century appears to be a period of a larger integration which has looked for mutual collaboration – with a few moments of staunch rivalry.

With both countries under military dictatorship in the 1960s and 1970s, the two nations were remarkably unfriendly towards one another. In the 1980s, there was growing economic and political cooperation; and since re-democratization, both countries have each day more built more bridges for local co-operation.

The Cisplatina war did not leave any profound or durable scars between Brazilians and Argentineans. Both peoples live together well. When the economic winds are in their favour, Argentineans go to Brazil, travel around, rent houses and buy everything. But when the wind turns, it's time for Brazilians to 'invade' Argentina.

Usually, Argentineans who can afford a reasonable holiday spend their summer in Brazil's southern beaches such as Florianópolis. On these beaches, there are specialised services for the Argentineans – stores and restaurants with Argentinean food, and even Spanish radio broadcasts.

There are many Brazilians living and working in Argentina, and the opposite is true as well. As Spanish speakers, Argentineans do not put much effort into learning Portuguese, as they can communicate well in Brazil. Interestingly, Brazilians can learn Spanish in an easier way. There are several Argentineans who live and work for their whole adult life in Brazil and do not speak Portuguese, but are perfectly adjusted.

Brazilian music is well-consumed in Argentina's nightlife, and the remarkable Argentinean ensemble Les Luthiers had huge success in Brazil during the 1970s. This iconic band, which used irony to sing about every aspect of everyday life, was adored in Brazil, even when they performed songs full of mockeries about the Brazilian way of life, satirizing Brazilian beaches, football and women.

During the first decade of the 2000s, however, Brazil took a prominent place not only in South America but also around the world. Brazil's rising economic power and growing international political presence undermined Argentina's intentions of regional leadership.

Argentineans, meanwhile, suffered for years from prolonged economic and social crises. Buenos Aires, their federal capital that was once called 'the Paris of South America', endured an incredible decay, and Argentina's social issues transformed that beautiful city into an unsafe place.

Yet cultural rivalries were always strongly accentuated between both countries, and the sports fields have been the perfect spot for these conflicts to emerge.

Since Argentineans have historically seen themselves as 'Europeans', and therefore superior to other South Americans, they cultivated a stereotype of overconfidence that has not disappeared throughout the years of social hardship.

Brazilian and Argentinean teams of any sport are always facing off against each other. In local South American tournaments or even playing for a spot in the Olympics or in international tournaments, a Brazil v Argentina derby is a battle where players always display extra energy. The rivalry is tremendous: one country may have a superior team, but the spirited fight is always there.

In the past few years, Argentineans have been better in sports such as basketball, while Brazil has dominated in volleyball. In women's sports, Brazilians have been beating the Argentineans in European Handball and football. For the men, both sports are competitive.

In men's football, the rivalry is enormous. The *Seleção* has a clear advantage of World Cup titles over the Argentinean team: five v two. On the other hand, Argentinean clubs have a better record in the Copa Libertadores da América (the South American version of the European Champions League). Argentina's two major teams (Independiente and Boca Juniors) have 13 trophies between them, while the biggest Brazilian winners (São Paulo and Santos) have only six.

Even with this rivalry, it's common that Brazilian teams sign Argentinean players. Great names such as goalkeeper Jose Poy, who played for São Paulo Futebol Clube in the 1950s and later became a coach of that team, or more recently, Carlos Tevez, are part of the Brazilian footballing world.

Argentineans have also made a contribution to other sports in Brazil. Recently, Ruben Magnano, the Argentinean basketball coach who won the gold medal with Argentina at the 2004 Athens Olympics, coached the Brazilian male basketball team for several years including in the Rio Olympics.

It is hard to play an Argentinean team in their headquarters. They provoke; they insult. Their 'European' arrogance has a dark side, such as the racist insults that prevail in their newspapers' headlines as soon as a Brazilian football team lands in Buenos Aires. 'The monkeys arrived', they stamp on their covers.

On the other hand, Argentinean nationalism has built a resilient people. Argentineans never give up. It is impressive how they can win a game even if they have a much inferior team. Their players in any sport learn from a young age that they have to put in everything. And they fight to their last drop of energy.

I also enjoy the way that Argentinean players are involved with their political causes.

The greatest Brazilian players are yet to show their strong support for important political and social issues in their country. On the other hand, just before the 2014 World Cup, Lionel Messi publicly supported the 'Abuelas de Plaza de Mayo' ('The grandmothers of the May Park') historical struggle. The 'Abuelas' is an NGO established by women who have been fighting for decades in order to know the whereabouts of their children and grandchildren who were kidnapped by the military during the dictatorship in Argentina.

The international press revived the South American rivalry, saying that Brazilians would 'die' for the second time in the World Cup if Argentina won the tournament. This was too generic and far beyond my own experience. During the World Cup, I saw plenty of social media pictures with my fellow Brazilians wearing the Argentinean jersey. Many Brazilians also did not care too much about the final World Cup game. Some supported Germany as they 'hate' Argentina, but many wanted their South American 'hermanos' (brothers) to win, so the trophy would remain in South America.

I supported Argentina in the 2014 World Cup final. I have plenty of Argentinean friends, and I admire their country and the way they cheer on their teams. And if there is something that the Germans have stolen from Brazil in the 2014 World Cup it was the pleasure to see a final between the two South Americans powerhouses. It would have been epic, not only on the field, but most of all on the stands.

I also supported Argentina because Germany had already won the World Cup three times – and if they win again, they would be dangerously close to Brazil with its five titles. Argentina has only two titles, so it could win and still be in a respectful distance from Brazil.

Unfortunately, my support was not enough, and Germany beat our South American *hermanos*! I was on their side, but there is one point where there is no argument: Pelé is greater than Maradona!

15.

Authentic learning, Brazilian teachers and the World Cup's education legacy

Miriam Balicas is a Brazilian citizen who lives and works in São Paulo. As with many other Brazilians in the lead-up to the World Cup, she was upset with Brazil's government and the tournament. She saw and felt that the average Brazilian urban resident's life conditions were becoming harder, leading to an explosive social situation on the streets. She became concerned.

Miriam is a committed Physical Education teacher who has been teaching for more than two decades within São Paulo's public educational system. Despite her bitter feelings towards the World Cup, she thought her students had the right to enjoy the tournament. She could appreciate how her students (aged between 11 and 15) were excited about having international football stars that they could only see on the internet or in their sticker albums in their own country.

Accordingly, Miriam's lessons in the months leading to the event incorporated the World Cup and all the potential themes that it mobilizes.

Brazil is a large country with more than 200 million inhabitants, hence its enormous education system. According to the 2012 national educational statistics, there are nearly 193,000 schools, where more than 50 million students are enrolled in the basic compulsory education years – years one to nine.

84% of students attend public schools, and 16% are in private schools. Municipality schools account for the majority of the public school enrolments (about 60%); Brazilian state schools account for 37% of public school enrolment, while just a few attend federal public schools.

Having every Brazilian child enrolled in a school was one of the major aims of the national education system during the 1990s and the 2000s. In addition to the basic aim of universal access to education – which is yet to be realised, as 3% of all Brazilian children still do not attend any school – Brazil's education system currently faces another challenge: achieving quality education as a right for every student in the public system.

It's within this context that the pedagogical practices that Miriam implemented within her school must be understood. In Miriam's view, the World Cup represented a chance to involve her students in a quality and authentic learning process that would help them to engage with their schooling process, and therefore support them to aim for further progress in their studies.

New buildings, disruptions, stadiums, incessant media coverage: Miriam knew how the World Cup invaded every sphere of hers and her students' lives. She realised that she should bring these daily issues and challenges presented by the World Cup to her school from the streets and mediate their understanding with her students.

Then, Miriam engaged the students in a cultural-sporting tournament called 'mini-World Cup'. Apparently, there were no big novelties. Children studied the World Cup countries' cultures and traditions, while playing an 'international' football tournament.

This education project was a dialogical process where the students could think critically about each participant country's history, culture and chances in the World Cup – while having fun.

Miriam's work was highlighted on the São Paulo's education department's website as evidence on how to engage students in authentic learning experiences and practices that brought 'the joy back to the school'.

Similar to Miriam's work – but targeting high school students in a private school – was the pedagogical work of Mildred Sotero. Also an enthusiastic Physical Education teacher who has worked for more than 20 years in São Paulo's private and public educational systems. Mildred's students engaged with an education project named 'Football Art'.

As the World Cup approached, Mildred wanted her students to learn about sport and football from several perspectives. She wanted them to develop a critical view about competitive sports. As a former athlete as well as a sport fan, she wanted to examine the connections between the sport and the entertainment industries, and how sport can be used as an oppressive tool to alienate people.

Mildred's lesson planning in the months before the event included a chance for her students to practice football and to develop their sporting skills. She not only wanted her students to deepen their understanding of the game's rules, tactics and strategies, but also to critically reflect on how the media can use sports news to manipulate ideologies and people.

Aside from being sports lovers and consumers, Mildred's aim was to develop critical citizens who could understand and even interfere in the political process of the sports realm.

To achieve these goals, Mildred used several pedagogical tools. She taught them new football skills within a game-based learning context. She saw how an inclusive, co-operative atmosphere – where the most skilful players taught the not- so-skilled ones – could positively operate to everyone's improvement. Mildred also included ballroom dancing classes in the students' activities, realizing that footballers must have dancing skills if they are to achieve 'football-art'.

Mildred also engaged her students with several media products and, as the World Cup approached, she understood the intensity of the media coverage – knowing that they would inevitably see or read something about the tournament. Therefore, she wanted her students not only to be consuming, but also critically analysing, all sorts of media messages.

Weekly, each student would produce a written report about the same media channel, trying to figure out the discursive changes it produced as the World Cup approached. Politics, streets demonstrations, social disruptions: everything was on the media's radar – and on Mildred's students' radar as well.

The World Cup had a huge impact in Brazilians' daily lives. From minor to major interventions, the World Cup's effects will linger across Brazil longer after the 'circus' has left the country.

These World Cup legacies go much further than the tangible ones such as stadiums and airports. They have a profound cultural and political meaning for the life of the host country and its citizens. Brazil will never be the same after the 'best World Cup ever'. As Brazil progresses to the next stage of its incipient democracy, the World Cup highlighted many of its social contradictions that urgently need solving.

Education systems must be alert and prepared to support their students with analysis and understanding of the World Cup's positive and negative effects in Brazil. New generations must learn how to live with the tournament's impacts. They have to thoughtfully consider these impacts so they can have an active voice in the future to decide whether Brazil should host the World Cup again or not.

Mildred's and Miriam's pedagogical practices were exemplary ways on how teachers, schools and education systems could use a mega sport event to achieve one of the most difficult but key elements in contemporary education. They engaged students in their school's lives to improve their social consciousness while having fun and enjoying themselves.

Could educators aim for a more commendable objective than this one?

16.

Will girls ever own the ball?
Women, football and gender legacy in Brazil

The launch of the photographic exhibition 'The ball's female owners' was one of the most socially relevant experiences in the months before the World Cup. The exhibition, displayed in an important cultural performing space in the heart of São Paulo, highlighted the work of 11 Brazilian female photographers who documented the "presence and the importance of women in football culture across the country", according to the exhibition's curator Diógenes Moura.

The exhibition, which later was released in a book of the same name, w a s full of football metaphors. From the number of photographers (11, as in a football team) to its name and contents, its organisers utilised words and images to question the gender order during the moment where "everything is running around the ball" in Brazil – as underlined by Diogenes Moura, in another football allegory.

Football metaphors pervade Brazilians' daily conversations – and not only during the World Cup. Football allegories are used in Brazilians' sporting lives, but also in their work or social life. You better be careful if you are 'on the penalty spot' in your job – they might kick you out. Your relationship can be in 'extra time', coming to an end, or even 'nil-all' if you are yet to have sex with your partner.

The 'ball's owner' is one of the most used football metaphors in daily Brazilian Portuguese language. The ball's owner is the one who has the power, or who is in charge of something. From the kid who holds the only ball in a group and will leave if his teammates don't play his way, to the boss who controls everything in the office, to the bouncer who says who comes in and out of the nightclubs – you better be friendly and keep an eye on the ball's owner.

However, the ball's owner is a male expression. That may sound weird to the monolingual English reader, but substantives in Portuguese have gender. For example, 'the table' (*a mesa*) is a female noun. 'The car' (*o carro*) is a male noun. One can say 'o dono', meaning the male owner, or 'a dona', meaning the female owner of something.

O dono da bola – the male ball's owner – has been traditionally used as a metaphor of the powerful men who control politics, business ... and football. Of course, the ball's owner works as a potent allegory as balls also symbolize phallic power, manliness and courage that allegedly only men have. The male ball's owner (*o dono da bola*) is really the one in command.

Therefore, by subverting the ball's ownership – by turning its possession to the women – the exhibition and book reminded the public that Brazilian women have made a significant contribution to the way the country plays. Women want to have a voice in celebrating Brazilians' way of life – *futebol*.

The enlargement of the 'ball's ownership' also assumes special significance when we look at Brazil's sports history to discover that women were officially forbidden to play football – amongst other 'no feminine' sports – from 1941 to 1979. The official sport sexist ban was implemented in 1941 by the National Sports Council after decades where all sorts of 'connoisseurs' were involved in civic arguments around the nature and limits of the feminine body.

As academic and football feminist activist Dr Silvana Goellner, from Universidade Federal do Rio Grande do Sul, points out, the 1941 Bill excluded women from participating in sports such as martial arts and football that were considered unsuitable for the 'female's body nature'.

The legislation was a death blow to an increasing number of female football teams that were appearing around Brazil.

Nevertheless, Brazilian women have always loved cheering and playing football – and they have been getting good results on the international stage as well. As soon as that sexist ban was lifted, many new teams were set up around Brazil.

Even facing large difficulties and harsh conditions, with no state or national championships, low wages, lots of social prejudice and managers' misogyny, Brazilian women have found a way into the world's top-level teams. They dominate the South American competitions, they have participated in every Olympic football tournament since women's football was introduced in the Summer Olympics in 1996, and they won Olympic silver medals in Athens 2004 and Beijing 2012.

The women's *Seleção* also did well in the 1999 US FIFA Women's World Cup (third Place) and were runners-up in the 2007 China FIFA Women's World Cup. Moreover, the Brazilian attacking midfielder Marta has been five times awarded FIFA World player of the year. This is a national record as she received this top prize more than any other male Brazilian player.

In the months leading to the World Cup, many people were afraid that the overwhelming male nature of the tournament was to worsen things for women's football in Brazil. However, civil society found ways to resist and fight for gender equality within Brazil's major cultural institution.

In the wake of the World Cup, exhibitions and debates were organised around Brazil with 'gender equality in football' as their central theme. Displays such as *'Futebol para a igualdade'* in the Museu da Republica in Rio de Janeiro aimed to retell women's football history in Brazil from their own perspective.

The interactive exhibition had also developed new ways for boys and girls to play football together, with no adult supervision or refereeing. Workshops and open lectures were organised so participants could learn how to use football as a tool to create a better and more inclusive world. In Porto Alegre, one of the World Cup host cities, the Centre for Sports Memory of the Universidade Federal do Rio Grande do Sul organised an exhibition to tell the history of women's football in Brazil.

This exhibition was an eye-opener for its visitors (school children and general population). It displayed photos and sports memorabilia from famous female players and newspapers articles that accounted for the late and recent history of female participation in the country's football landscape. The retrospective reminded visitors of the huge but invisible presence that women have always had in Brazil's football history.

The chair of this exhibition, Dr Silvana Goellner, of Universidade Federal do Rio Grande do Sul, argued that it's on the streets and in educational projects – funded by federal and local governments or by NGOs – where it's possible to see the growing visibility of girls 'owning the ball'. They want to participate in the football world, and they will fight for it. They will not wait anymore, they will make things happen.

Women's professional football might still be overshadowed in Brazil not only by the overwhelming presence of men's football, but also by a continuing misogynistic mentality with its historical roots. However, as Juliana Cabral, the 2004 Brazilian Olympic team captain and silver medallist once declared:

The girls don't need to have the same amount of money as the boys have; we know this is a corrupted industry, and we don't want to take part in this dirty world; but we do want to play our football with dignity.

Juliana's cry was an isolated call for change in the sports world. As the exhibitions and social projects have demonstrated, this would not happen from 'football wishful thinking'. Instead, it will require a huge fight to transform conservative mentalities. But Brazilian women – and their supporters – are ready for this battle.

17.

Professor Felipão's pedagogies or when the family did not show up for Christmas

Luiz Felipe Scolari, or just Scolari as he is internationally known, was the *Seleção's* coach for Brazil's World Cup. In Brazil, he is known as Felipão. In Portuguese, the ending '*ão*' is frequently used to express that something is really big. After a proper name, it means also to be cheerful, or used to affectionately refer to someone. Felipão, or 'Big Felipe', is a big guy, not only because of his size, but mainly because of his macho manners; he talks and walks the hegemonic male way.

Branded as a tough coach who had many troubles with the media in the past – he allegedly punched a journalist during a media conference after a Palmeiras' training session in 1998 – Felipão mastered his coaching job on the sidelines, coaching small and middle-size clubs in Brazil's South and Northeast before reaching greener pastures.

As a player he was fierce despite not being a skilful defender. He also never played for a top league club, but as an aggressive centre-back, he learned how to observe games from his own penalty box. His team leadership abilities were developed under harsh conditions as observed in some of the tournaments he played in the Rio Grande do Sul or in the Alagoas states.

Most of all, he learned that to succeed in the football realm, one has to be the first to 'throw the first punch' – and this was remarkably consistent throughout his career, until reaching the World Cup in 2014.

Coming from humble origins, Felipão completed a university degree as a Physical Education teacher and began coaching in the early 1980s. He was successful in his first season as the head coach of the CSA, winning the Alagoas state championship in 1982. During the 1980s, he coached middle-size clubs in Rio Grande do Sul as well as spending a few years coaching in Middle Eastern countries, with a highlight of winning the Gulf Cup as the head coach of Kuwait's National Team.

His first big spell at a Brazilian team was as head coach of *Grêmio Football Porto Alegrense*, one of the two top teams in Rio Grande do Sul state and a club of national relevance. Felipão started to gain fame as a coach in the country after winning the 1987 Rio Grande do Sul state championship (the 'Gauchão', one of the toughest regional tournaments in Brazil). His reputation grew as he then conquered the Brazil Cup in 1991 with Criciuma FC, a modest club from Santa Catarina, another Southern state.

It was in his second spell in Grêmio that Felipão saw his career reach higher levels: with the club he won the 1994 Brazil Cup, the 1995 Libertadores Cup (Copa Libertadores da América) and the 1996 Brazilian Championship (the 'Brasileirão'), as well as several state championships. He led the club to the FIFA Club World Cup (then known as Intercontinental Cup), losing the match between the Copa Libertadores champion and the European Cup winner (the Dutch club Ajax) in a penalty shootout.

Felipão was heavily labelled by the national football press (mainly in Rio de Janeiro and in São Paulo) as a *'retranqueiro'*, a coach who 'parked the bus' in defense. The gossip was that he asked his teams to perform violent tackles on the opponent's players' legs.

He was largely targeted by media for not adopting a *jogo bonito* style; instead, famous sporting journalists accused him of playing the opposite to this style, unaffectionately known as the *'jogo feio'* – the dreadful game. However, Grêmio's fans have fond memories of Felipão as he was one of the most successful coaches in the club's history.

In 1997, Felipão took another step up on his way to national stardom. After spending a year as coach of Jubilo Iwata (a Japanese club), he returned to Brazil to start coaching Palmeiras, one of the most traditional and historic clubs in the country. In the same year, under Felipão, the club was vice-champion of the 'Brasileirão'. In the following year, despite being heavily criticised in the media, he won the Brazil Cup, the Copa Mercosul (the first continental title in Palmeiras' history). A few months later in 1999, Felipão's Palmeiras won for the first time their long-dreamt title: the Copa Libertadores da América.

Despite the intense media criticism, Felipão started to see his name constantly cited as a potential coach for the *Seleção*.

Felipão, though, did not sit back on his recently acquired fame. He continued to work hard, leading Palmeiras to another Copa Libertadores da América final in 2000 (where he lost to the Argentinean giant, Boca Juniors), among other titles. He then moved to Cruzeiro, another major club from Minas Gerais state where, after successive positive campaigns and titles, he received a call to get his first spell as the *Seleção's* coach.

The year was 2001 and the *Seleção* was under the terrible threat of, for the first time in its history, not being able to qualify for a World Cup tournament, this time to be hosted in South Korea and Japan in 2002.

Felipão led Brazil to its 'compulsory' World Cup's spot to the 2002 World Cup competition.

However, the *Seleção's* performances in the qualifying matches were not convincing. To add more misery to Felipão's woefulness, the team lost to Honduras and left that year's Copa America in an early stage of the tournament. Then, to complete the rough scenario, there was the Romário episode, where once again the coach was severely criticised by national media.

However, the *Seleção's* coach was confident in what he was doing.

On his path to success, he learned one or two things about media dealings. He was clearly friendlier towards reporters, mainly the ones from the influential Rede Globo, the main Brazilian broadcaster.

However, he never changed his personal values. He carried as a badge of honour the fact that he was a graduated Physical Education teacher with a university degree; his conception of the teaching profession was that, more than someone to deliver content, students needed someone to talk and to listen to them.

He transferred this notion to his coaching style. He felt that his players needed a fatherly figure. It was this paternal style, mixing affection, respect and control that granted him the trust of the *Seleção* leaders – players such as Ronaldo, Rivaldo, Cafu and Roberto Carlos, who in 2002 were already legendary international stars.

The small talk is that these players did not want Romário in the team, and that Felipão made a deal with them: he would not call Romário, but they would have to leave their heart on the field at the World Cup. However, this story was consistently denied by those accused of being involved.

Without Romário, Felipão built the team in his own manner. He created a familial atmosphere, as he believed this was the best way for the team to flourish. Felipão's family (*the família Felipão*) became a legend in the country. They were really committed to each other throughout the 2002 competition, resulting in them winning the title.

When Felipão returned to coach the team for the 2014 Brazil World Cup, and after winning the 2013 Confederations Cup, the media and the country celebrated the revival of the *família Felipão*. Unfortunately, though, the context was incomparable.

The home ground advantage was lost due to bad planning and because of the enormous pressure of playing at home. Unlike Teixeira, who was forced to leave the CBF's presidency two years before the World Cup due to his association in football bribery scandals, the new president, Jose Maria Marin – also now incarcerated by the US authorities on charges of corruption – enjoyed being involved with the team and voicing his ideas about which players should be on the coach's list. There was even more small politics to be played with this type of mismanagement.

In Portuguese, the word *professor* means 'teacher' (the last syllable is stressed, to say profe**ssor**). It is common that students call their teachers as *professor* followed by their first name. 'Professor Jorge, I have a question', my students used to say to me when I taught in Brazilian universities. They may just say 'Hi, *professor*'.

In the football milieu, it is also normal that players call their coaches as *professor* – meaning teacher – followed by the name by which they are usually known. This might be only their first or their last name.

In 2002, professor Felipão's familial plans worked well and he ended up as a World Cup champion coach. However, differing from 2002, the 2014 players needed much more than hugs and control from their *professor*. They needed tactical lessons and strategic direction, which the *familia* scheme was not capable of providing.

Without crucial content to deliver to his players, Felipão's fatherly figure actually lost their respect. The old *professor* could not engage his class in his lessons anymore; the dialogue between the coach and the team was broken. Felipão stopped talking to his team which, consequently, lost its direction.

The 2014 school term ended up earlier than in professor Felipão's planned calendar. The *familia* did not show up for Christmas anymore. This time, the celebration was silent and sad: the only noise that was heard were the seven goals Germany scored v. the *Seleção* in the semi-final.

18.

The Seleção's camp: why should we practice?

Together with the 'football-land' myth, or perhaps influenced by this 'myth', there is a widespread misconception that the Seleção never trained enough for any World Cup. Despite some blind support, even within the mainstream media still arguing that Brazilian players are the world's best and only by entering the pitch the opponents would fear them, the evidence shows that the Seleção usually prepares well for World Cup tournaments.

For example, before the 1958 World Cup, the selected players were given the best medical attention available in that period. Interestingly, the diseases that were the primary focus for the Seleção's medical crew were the ones that plagued the overall Brazilian population: parasites and anaemia.

Moreover, players' oral health was extensively cared for and nearly 300 teeth were extracted from their mouths collectively, either to treat existing cavities and to prevent potential infections during the competition. Additionally, Brazilian players were treated for syphilis, another prevalent illness among footballers of that time.

Paulo Machado de Carvalho, the head of the 1958 Brazilian team, and the Seleção's management group were so worried about how the players' sexual activities could negatively impact on their on-field performances that they demanded the Seleção's host hotel replace every female staff member with a male one. It is worth noting that the chosen hotel was nominated after an extensive scouting process that scrutinised more than 20 hotels in Sweden.

The 1958 planning is just an example that the norm for CBF (and the previous sporting bodies that managed national footballing teams) has always been to offer the best preparation possible for the *Seleção*. Management always knew how valuable the team is for the nation – and for them. Before and during international competitions, players have access to excellent training, medical and facility conditions. They are treated as national heroes.

A few times, though, the players' stardom combined with commercial interests have jeopardised the team's preparations. This was the case of the 2006 World Cup played in Germany.

Brazil won the previous World Cup in 2002 in Korea/Japan so, under the FIFA rules at the time, the title holder did not have to play in the qualifying games, having already a guaranteed spot in the next World Cup finals. The then head coach, Parreira, who was again at the top *Seleção's* job after coaching the winning side of the 1994 World Cup, called several 2002 'heroes' alongside other famous players to line-up for the team.

However, that proved to be a catch-22 situation for the coach and the team, as key players like Ronaldo and Adriano presented themselves overweight and not in peak fitness condition. Parreira decided to trust on their 'magic' even if they clearly lacked playing condition. Furthermore, the CBF sold tickets to the training facilities of the team for people to watch the training sessions.

As a consequence, the training sessions were constantly interrupted by fans and sponsors looking for photos, autographs and even harassing players for their jerseys, shorts or any other apparel. In addition, and in clear contrast to what had happened in previous World Cups, Parreira could not control the team's stars, so the core players left the hotel every night to party until dawn.

So in contrast to previous World Cup tournaments, and subsequent ones, the 2006 preparations cannot be seen as the normal model for Brazil. Usually the *Seleção* has professional and well-thought-out training camps before and during the competition.

With a home World Cup in sight, the CBF planned for the best arrangements ever to be given to the team. The CBF training headquarters, known as Granja Comary, received a luxurious revamp worth millions of dollars. Indoor amenities were deemed fantastic and private by the players and team's staff. The Granja Comary also had good football pitches and other training facilities, a brand new gym, medical rooms, restaurants and everything needed for a five-star preparation for the team. However, a few details escaped the management team.

First, the location. Despite having great training and accommodation facilities for the team and its staff, the Granja Comary is located in the city of Teresópolis. With a two-hour travel distance from Rio de Janeiro airport, Teresópolis is situated in a mountainous region where temperatures drop low during June and July, which is winter time in Brazil and when the World Cup was played.

This location forced the players to face several hours of bus traveling to and from Rio's airport, plus the flying times to the host city where the match was played, which could be anything up to six hours. In addition, there was the temperature change that could go from 40 Celsius degrees in one day playing in Fortaleza (Brazil's northeast) to 5 Celsius degrees on the next day returning to Teresópolis.

The team indeed had peace of mind while in their Granja Comary's indoor facilities. However, when on the field, there were nearly 1,000 journalists from around the world covering the *Seleção*'s every movement. There were days when the team's training was interrupted by Rede Globo (the main Brazilian broadcaster which has several broadcasting deals signed with the CBF) so their journalists could interview players interacting with their TV shows' characters, as just one example.

To make things worse, a few years earlier in 2011, the Teresópolis area had suffered a major 'natural' disaster. Thousands of precarious dwellings that hung from the hills were dragged by severe torrents and hundreds of the region's inhabitants disappeared in the calamity. Many children who lost families in this tragedy, as well as other vulnerable citizens of the region, were granted permission to attend the Seleção's training sessions.

The players, mostly with humble origins, knew how important it was to offer some relief to these people. However, the timing of these visits was not well planned. Players became extremely touched by listening to all their visitors' sad stories, to the extent that a clear humanitarian mission of offering comfort and support for the disaster's victims disrupted the team's preparation.

As the tournament progressed and entered in its final stages, more people started to attend the Granja Comary. International correspondents were looking for any new angle to report on the Seleção. The CBF's president's friends and sponsors were granted access to the players and staff. Even opposing national team's observers were reported to be found at Granja Comary to spy on the team's tactical trainings. Felipão was not afforded any secrecy on his trainings.

The Seleção, despite qualifying for the tournament's knockout stages, was not playing the type of quality football demanded by supporters and the media. The pressure was mounting as influential Brazilian journalists constantly criticised the team and its coach.

An incident between the coach and famous journalists shows how the team's preparations were disturbed by the troubled atmosphere at Granja Comary.

As more than 700 journalists gathered in the Granja Comary's press facilities, the Seleção's press attaché entered the room and, pointing to just a handful of Brazilian media professionals, asked them to go inside for a private meeting with the team's coach. As reported by these seven chosen journalists, an agitated Felipão wanted to gather their opinions about what was going wrong with the team.

Moreover, the coach disclosed to them that he was happy with all his players but one, and that he regretted having this player in the team. Even though the coach never disclosed this player's name, his comment gave room for numerous speculations in the press and clearly damaged even further the ties between players and coach.

The outcome of this secret meeting was terrible. The majority of the journalists who were not called to participate wrote angry reports about this event. The few in attendance had no confidentiality obligations so they reported on what they saw and heard.

Instantly, internet and newspaper headlines reported about that meeting – from the coach's lack of self-confidence to rumours of the player who should not be there according to their own coach. The news was not looking good for the team.

Then, the fatal blow to the team came when Felipão was forced to choose a replacement for Neymar, due to the star's serious injury in the quarter finals match.

Neymar was clearly the team's best player and the whole team's strategy revolved around him.

The Seleção's leaders approached their coach and argued that the only way to face Germany in the semi-final would be to adopt a defensive style. Despite his players' advice, Felipão did not change his tactics and, after a brief 30 minute training session, he chose Bernard to replace Neymar.

In that period, Bernard was barely making it on the bench at his Ukrainian club. Yet, the coach, with a 'football-land myth' fashioned argument and a 'football wishful thinking' approach, declared that Bernard had 'magical legs' and that he was more than suitable to be Neymar's replacement.

For the *Seleção*, the combination of 'football land' mythological beliefs and commercial interests proved to be fatal in the 2014 World Cup.

19.

The Argentinean lesson

The 2014 World Cup taught several lessons to Brazilian football both on and off the field. However, a few of these lessons may never be totally assimilated by Brazil's football stakeholders.

Broadcasters, clubs and most particularly the CBF, may continue to insist on pathways that evidently are jeopardizing the development of the game in this football-country. Political and economic powers will certainly dismiss the value of important international practices that should have been learned during the World Cup to help renovate Brazilian football.

However, one lesson that was clearly learned by Brazilians during the World Cup came from somewhere they did not expect at all. The cheering lesson from their Argentinean *hermanos*.

Argentinean sporting people are strong competitors. They never give up regardless of the hardship presented by the opponents. This ideology also applies to their supporters. Argentinean supporters never turn their back on their teams. It doesn't matter whether they are winning, drawing or far behind in the score: they cheer forever more.

Argentineans are one of the loudest and most loyal supporters' groups in the world. As supporters, they are far better than the Brazilians, who easily turn their back on their teams.

The *Seleção* has never received the type and level of support that the Argentinean team has, throughout both team's histories. Despite loving their team, Brazilians are too critical and do not act as blinded supporters. This is even truer in some regions of the country compared with others.

The *Seleção* players usually dislike playing in São Paulo city, as they are regularly booed by impatient supporters after just a few minutes of not finding a goal scoring opportunity. An example of this tense relationship was during a World Cup qualifying game in 2000 when the *Seleção* was playing against Colombia.

With several difficulties in finding any space in the Colombian defensive system, the team was not creating any scoring opportunities or putting on a good footballing performance. Around the 60th minute the fans in the packed Morumbi stadium started to boo non-stop towards the team.

Supporters were throwing small Brazilian flags on the pitch and did not stop the protests even though the *Seleção* scored a winner in the last few minutes of the game.

Argentineans would never do that against their own team. They may protest against the manager or some player, but not while their team is playing. The 90 minutes of a football match are sacred and you should only support your team during this time. Argentineans use the game time to chant loudly and to really promote a party on the stands, displaying a magnificent and unique football cheering culture.

These different supporting styles were clear in the 2014 World Cup. While Argentineans arrived in Brazil with a range of football chants that they performed inside stadiums, on public transport and everywhere they partied, Brazilian supporters did not provide a great deal of chanting. They sang their national anthem, but remained quiet on the stands for most of the match. A few times they echoed a boring chant about being proud Brazilians, but even that did not last more than a few minutes and was not chanted by everyone with passion.

One explanation for this behaviour can be found in the divided social classes and their experience with football supporting culture. This culture looks to be spread across all social classes in Argentina, and nearly every Argentinean learns how to properly cheer on their team. This is particularly the case from a young age, when Argentineans learn the specific chants of their family team and of their national team.

This cheering culture seems not to be wide spread in Brazil, staying restricted to the people who regularly attend local football matches and in which the '*torcidas organizadas*', the active support groups of Brazilian football, draw their members from. The cheering culture was clearly not embedded amongst the Brazilian upper classes who were the people who could afford to attend the expensive World Cup matches.

It seems that the ordinary and more popular Brazilian football supporters, the ones who sing and support their team non-stop, did not find their way inside the World Cup stadiums. This fact shows once more the great cultural barriers between Brazilian social classes as reflected in the football culture of the country.

Argentineans from all walks of life made their way to Brazil during the World Cup. In the southern Brazilian state that borders Argentina (Rio Grande do Sul), there were camping facilities to accommodate 'hinchas' (supporters) from Argentina and from other South American countries.

On the other hand, Brazilian and Argentinean police exchanged information about the feared '*barra bravas*', the Argentinean 'hooligans'. Drawing upon this intel, there were nearly 2,000 *barra bravas* who were not allowed to enter Brazil during the World Cup. Nevertheless, some of them, like the feared *Independiente barra brava* leader Bebote (Pablo Alvarez) tricked the police, entered Brazil and attended a few World Cup matches; a few times he was disguised as an European supporter, but at other times he did not cover his face and even used social media to post his photos inside World Cup stadiums, celebrating his victories over the security systems.

The lessons that Argentineans *hinchas* brought to Brazil were quickly adopted by the locals. The provocative Argentinean chants were appropriated and turned around by Brazilian supporters on the streets and on social media. Brazilians were clever enough to mix the Argentinean and Brazilian rhythms to respond to their South American *hermanos'* provocations in a comic way.

Using Brazil's overwhelming world footballing record over Argentine (five World Cups against Argentina's two), Brazilians mocked their opponents in a constructive style. Maradona and Pelé were constantly cited and compared in the chants, each side trying to leverage their idols' achievements to their own benefit. Images of a Copacabana beach packed with Brazilian and Argentinean supporters, each crowd responding in a humorous manner to the other groups' chants, were a highlight of the World Cup.

The Argentinean lesson also showed that, even with all the commodification embedded in today's football realm, supporters on the streets proved that football is still the people's game.

20.

Hey, Dilma, shove it up?

Thursday, June 12, 2014. The special day of the opening ceremony of the World Cup had finally arrived! After countless controversies over public expenditure on 'FIFA standard' football stadiums instead of on public health and education, after protesters hit the streets of the country in the previous year, and on the eve of the tournament, the great day was finally here.

Despite all the polemics and questions raised by international and local media, which stated that Brazil would never complete the stadiums on time and all other necessary works for the tournament, the opening ceremony was about to commence in the Arena Corinthians and Brazil would host its second World Cup.

Whenever the Seleção plays a World Cup match, the streets of the main cities of the country become empty. A foreigner who is in Brazil during a World Cup being played abroad who tries to go to a bank branch or to access any public service would definitely be lost and wondering what had happened, as everything shuts down. Courts, universities, schools, shops, everyone is watching 'the match'.

In the 20th century, it was nearly customary that work arrangements included an informal holiday during the Seleção's World Cup games. More recently, new provisions to watch the matches were introduced in schools, universities and work places – either students or workers were dismissed a few hours prior to the matches so they could go home and watch it with family and friends, or the work place, the school or the university would organise a big screen so regular activities could be stopped during 'the match' and everyone would gather to watch it.

Either way, the atmosphere surrounding a Seleção's match, particularly during a World Cup, is always celebratory. People organise small parties and barbeques at friends' and family's places, or even at work places, so everyone can have fun while cheering for the 'motherland in boots'.

For the 2014 World Cup played at home, things were no different. Despite the critiques and the frustration with FIFA and the World Cup organisers, at the end of the day, millions of Brazilians wanted to cheer on the team and to party with friends and families – or just to enjoy another holiday.

The World Cup General Bill, pushed by FIFA, went through the Brazilian Parliament and was signed off by President Dilma. It allowed the Federal, State and local governments to call a holiday any time that the *Seleção* was to play, or in the course of any other major game during the event. Host cities were particularly encouraged to call for a local holiday to lessen the chaotic traffic conditions and to benefit the matches' attendees and the general population who would be looking for somewhere to watch 'the match'.

It was a public holiday on that 12th of June in São Paulo and a packed Arena Corinthians was about to host the 2014 FIFA World Cup opening game between Brazil and Croatia. Before that, of course, the opening ceremony was to entertain the local and the global audiences, showcasing some aspects of Brazilian culture and sending a message for world peace and unity.

The mandatory symbolisms of Brazilian nature were presented, with the representation of the magnificence that is the Amazon rainforest. Dancers showed the diverse Brazilian cultural traditions, from Germanic inspired pair dances to more energetic Carnaval rhythms such as the *samba* and the *frevo*. *Capoeira*, the Brazilian martial arts was also performed, and teenagers from local clubs displayed some football skills to demonstrate Brazil's passion for the sport.

The Ceremony ended with musical stars Jennifer Lopez, Pitbull and Claudinha Leitte singing 'We are one (Ole Ola)', the official 2014 FIFA World Cup Song.

An important part of the opening ceremony unfortunately went nearly unnoticed by the local and international audience. A young paraplegic woman wearing an exoskeleton created by the Brazilian neuroscientist Miguel Nicolelis's team, did the official World Cup kickoff using just her mind to control her vest. Her symbolic act was not highlighted by the ceremony's broadcasters.

However, what was well emphasised around the world was the behaviour of a section of Brazilian supporters towards Dilma Roussef, the then president of Brazil. Just after the national anthem, these supporters moved in the direction of the tribune where Roussef and FIFA authorities were and started to scream: 'Ei, Dilma, vai tomar no cu!'; 'Hey, Dilma, shove it up!'.

Booing authorities in public events is a normal part of Brazilian civic life. During the 2007 Rio Panamerican Games, when Brazil was kicking off its mega sports events era, the then president Lula was booed as other authorities had been booed in different occasions in the past. Even in the World Cup Opening Ceremony, FIFA authorities such as its then president, Joseph Blatter, were booed. In a mix of protest and fun, Brazilians enjoy demonstrating their revolt towards authorities by booing them at official international events.

However, in the 2014 World Cup opening match, the type of protest was different and raised questions about the future cohesion of Brazil's social fabric. The president was not only booed, but the spectators were ferociously aggressive towards her.

Importantly, the name calling started and was predominant in a VIP area of the stadium. The supporters who were seated there had paid for the most expensive tickets or, in most cases, were invited guests of the country's largest private bank, which of course was rewarding its richest customers with these privileged tickets and seating places.

There is a large distance between the traditional booing as a mixed demonstration of fun and revolt, and the 'new' name calling practice inaugurated in the World Cup's opening match. The name calling against the country's president opened several questions about Brazil's social context, including the prevalence of a *machista* mentality represented in the temple of the country's male power: the football arena.

Would a male president endure such verbal aggressions? Was it not a coincidence that as a woman, Dilma was the first president to suffer the escalation of public protests, from a 'civilised' booing to a hostile and violent cursing?

In Brazil's national calendar, June 12th is Valentine's Day. In 2014, it also marked the day when presenting flowers to women on that romantic occasion was replaced by blaspheming a former guerrilla, mother and grandmother who had the courage to challenge the political gender status quo to become the first woman to be elected president of Brazil.

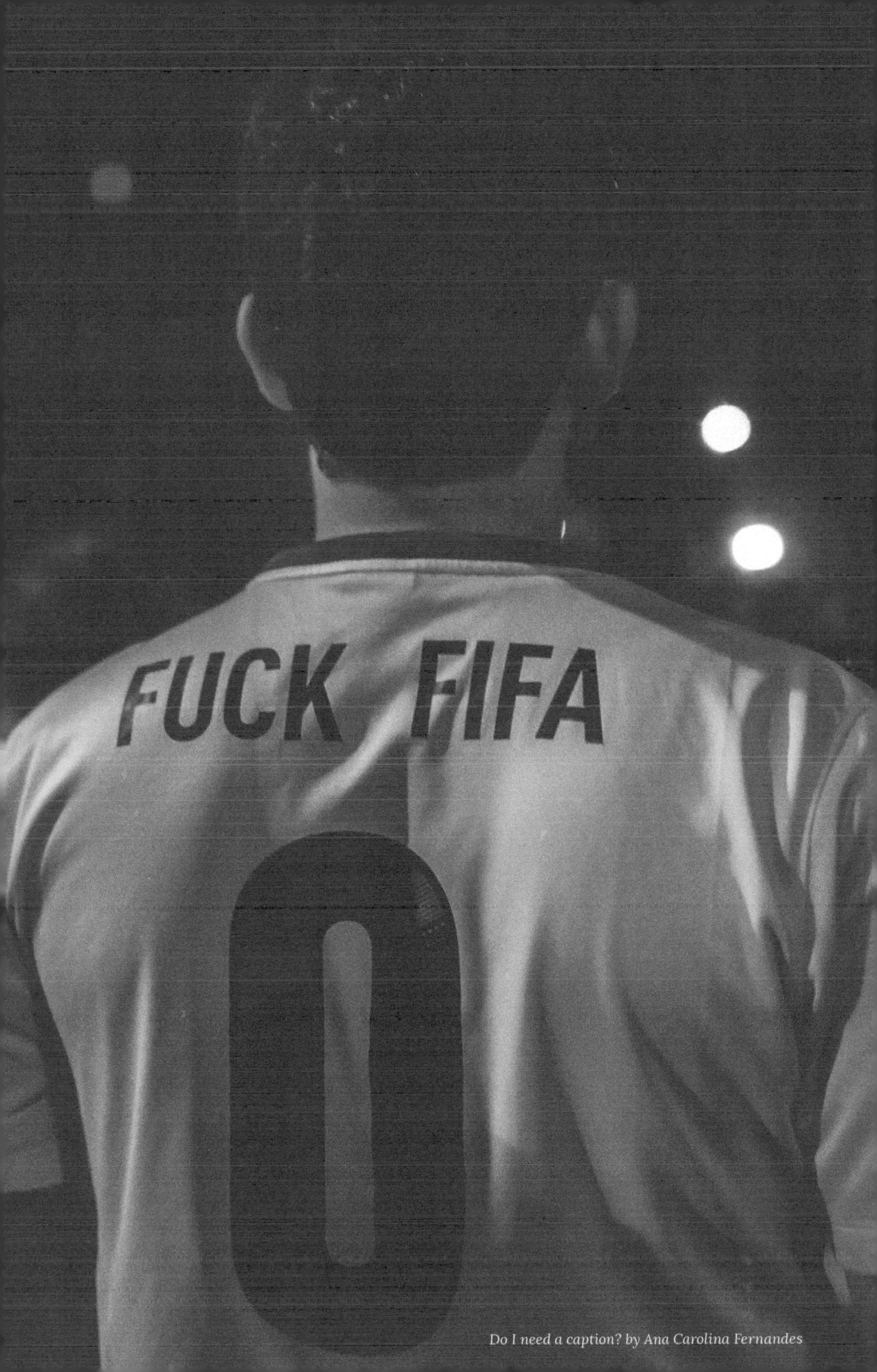

Do I need a caption? by Ana Carolina Fernandes

Genuine Futebol-arte by Luciana Whitaker

Whose World Cup? by Ana Carolina Fernandes.

Rio Revolution Rock, by Ana Carolina Fernandes

We love the Seleção!
by Lulu di Mello

The World Cup funeral
by Ana Carolina Fernandes

PART 3:
The after match —
what kind of legacy?

21.

Brazilians all let us rejoice:
FIFA arrests and a new era for world football?

When the first news talking about the FIFA arrests came up in late May 2015, I thought I was back in 1938, listening to Orson Welles broadcasting his famous radio drama 'The War of the Worlds'. Just like Welles' listeners, it took me a while to believe in what I was hearing, reading and watching on every mainstream or social media channel.

The news looked like another fake alien invasion on Earth. However, after following the media frenzy, I realised that everything was real: a handful of top-level football officials had just been arrested in Switzerland, on the brink of FIFA's meeting to elect its new president.

Amongst the ones arrested, there was Jose Maria Marin, the former president and, at the time of his arrest in May 2015, deputy president of the Brazilian Football Federation (CBF).

The question that the world wanted to know was: who is Marin? How did an octogenarian man, with clear links to the military dictatorship that tortured and killed countless Brazilians, with connections to corrupted operations, hold such a powerful position?

Marin was a politician who had always been associated with the right wing. In 1971, he was elected as a state representative by the government party then – ARENA. That was one of the darkest periods of the military running in Brazil. A few years earlier, all political parties had been extinguished, and then replaced by only two parties: ARENA, the civil face of the militaries, and MDB, which brought together the government oppositionists who had not been arrested, tortured, killed or sent to overseas exile.

As a politician, Marin was always keen to show his loyalty to the military as far as they left him near to the safe-deposit box. He was also close to an infamous and sadistic torturer, the chief commissioner Sergio Fleury. Marin, as a state representative, was always ready to jump on the state parliament stage to deliver hate speeches against 'communists' – and the authoritarian government just loved it.

Marin's most infamous speech in the state parliament stage was in 1975 and led to the imprisonment, torture and murder of Vladimir Herzog, a journalist who was in charge of the São Paulo state broadcaster, TV *Cultura*. Herzog had come back to Brazil that year, after fleeing the country a few years before with his wife and two young sons to work in London as a journalist for BBC.

Then, in 1975 Marin delivered a speech in the state parliament which was seen as the green light for the military secret police to arrest, torture and kill Herzog.

Marin's speech accused the state broadcaster for not supporting the government in its broadcasting as they should be. Marin blamed TV *Cultura* of being infiltrated by 'communists'. A week after Marin's speech, Herzog was 'invited' to go to the headquarters of the secret police – where they inflicted him with such brutal torture that he passed away. Quickly, the military broadcast that his murder was 'suicide' – a version that was hard to believe on.

A few years later, in 1978, the Federal Judge Marcio Jose de Moraes condemned the Brazilian state for the illegal incarceration, torture and murdered of Vladimir Herzog. In 1996, the Federal Government Special Committee for the Political Disappeared during the dictatorship officially acknowledged that Herzog was murdered during his incarceration and offered an indemnification to his family. The family denied the monies and demanded the truth. Nobody has yet been arrested for his murder.

In 1978, Marin was appointed by the military as the deputy-governor of São Paulo state – free elections were yet to come back to the country's civic life. Four years later, when Paulo Maluf, the then governor of São Paulo, left his position run for president of the country which was still governed by João Figueiredo, a military president, Marin was the state governor for 10 months. This position put him closer to the safe and all the riches it contained than ever before. According to sports journalist Juca Kfouri, Marin once said that, "it's impossible to be São Paulo's governor and not become rich".

Marin has always been involved with sports, more precisely, football. He was the president of the São Paulo Football Federation, one of the richest and most powerful sporting bodies in Brazil, and he was the head of the of the Brazilian delegation which played in the 1986 Mexico World Cup.

Then, when he was aiming for an easy life as deputy-president of the Brazilian Football Federation, things in the football world turned upside down – but in Marin's favour. In 2012, after 23 years in control of the Brazilian Football Federation, Ricardo Teixeira was forced to resign from his position as he was facing a wave of corruption accusations internationally.

Teixeira fled the country, and Marin, as the CBF's senior deputy president, inherited Teixeira's positions in the Brazilian football realm. He became not only the new CBF's president at age 80, but also president of the 2014 World Cup local organising committee. Marin was back in power in a big way.

Marin has plenty of episodes that demonstrate his character. Some of the biggest moments are hilarious. Like in 2012, when he gained the nickname of 'Johnny Medallion': as he presented the medals to the winners of the Under-21 São Paulo Cup, the most prestigious football tournament for that age group in Brazil, Marin was caught by the cameras pocketing a few medals that were to be handed to the young players, who are still waiting for their award.

Unfortunately, Marin's life stories are far worse than this comic event. As CBF president as well as the World Cup 'top-man' he was not only receiving high wages, he was in charge of all sponsorship and broadcasting deals, stadiums constructions and more. Hence, he was close to the safe-deposit box again, which appears to be his favourite work spot.

The embarrassment of the Brazilian president, Dilma Roussef, was visible at any World Cup ceremonies or matches where she had to be side by side with Marin. She had been tortured by the military, and he was a big soldier in the perpetrators' side.

Vladimir Herzog's oldest son, Ivo, had also tried to convince FIFA to demote Marin from his position in charge of the Local Organising Committee. He organised an online petition with thousands of signatures and delivered it to FIFA's headquarters – but he did not get any answer from Sepp Blatter's men.

Marin was also responsible for the camp where the Brazilian team was staying during the competition. Marin ordered a multi-million dollar renovation of the CBF facilities in Teresópolis just before the World Cup and determined that the *Seleção* would be staying there during the tournament.

There were days, on the eve of important games, that there were more than 1,000 people watching the *Seleção*'s practices: no privacy to train, no secrecy, and a noisy environment. But Marin was happy as sponsors were pleased to be close to the team, and Rede Globo's journalists had exclusive time to talk to the players.

Early in 2015, when his term as CBF's president was ending, Marin, in a smart move, exchanged positions with his most loyal deputy, Marco

Del Nero, who became CBF's president until the end of 2017 when he was suspended by FIFA because of the US FIFA trials. A few months before being arrested, Marin went back to his deputy role at CBF – but kept his position at the 2016 Rio Olympics as the chairman of the FIFA competition – and until his arrest still had a tremendous office in the luxurious CBF headquarters at Rio de Janeiro, a huge building in the heart of the city that he has named after... Jose Maria Marin...

Fortunately, Marin was finally caught in Zurich and extradited to the US in 2015 to face several corruption charges. Later on, following FIFA's guidelines, CBF temporarily dismissed Marin from their directive boards, and removed his name from the building.

Brazilians rejoiced when Marin was finally convicted and incarcerated in a US Federal prison. At least the Brazilians who could see the inseparable ties between lack of social democracy, authoritarian government and corruption.

At the end of the day, Orson Welles' metaphor was appropriate for this case: two worlds have faced and battled each other during the 2014 Brazil World Cup. On one side, the businessmen and the politicians who took over the country to run their competition and make their dollars. On the other side the people who had to pay for it.

In a rare scenario, the 'aliens' went to jail, giving hope to the people that things were slowly starting to change in the football world. Should we be optimistic about football's future?

22.

From Dunga to Tite:
is the Seleção worth a devil's kiss?

The *Seleção*'s defeat in the 2014 World Cup semi-final was shocking.

The appalling defeat v. Germany was outrageous not only because of its final score but also because of the team's and coaching staff's reactions during and after the match. The football world could not believe what was going on in the first half where the *Seleção* suffered five goals in just a few minutes. Supporters were leaving the stadium or just turned off their TVs.

Felipão, who was always known as a coach with a large bag of tricks, did nothing to calm the team down; he just remained seated on the bench, looking at the game without trying anything to stop the carnage. In the second half, a few players who were substituted during the match were standing in the coach's technical area giving instructions to their teammates. The scene was dreadful.

After that, and in some sort of denial, Felipão declared that the result was due to "five-minutes of a mental blank" by the team. Besides that, he said he could not see any mistakes with the team's tactics and strategies for that game. Brazil went to the third place play-off match against the Netherlands, with the *Seleção* again in shambles, where had another defeat. Not only was the score humiliating (3-0 at home) but the team also did not show any desire to win or any reaction, showing an unbelievable lack of emotional balance.

Despite these shameful defeats at home, Felipão firmly believed that the CBF's president, Jose Maria Marin, would honour his word and would keep him as the *Seleção*'s coach just after the World Cup. After all, according to him, everything was fine and the losses were explicable because of the absence of an injured Neymar and secondly, for the "five-minute mental blank".

He completed a full report of the team under his supervision and thought that he would have a chance to meet Marin in the CBF's headquarters for a full debrief of the World Cup as well as plans to start preparing for 2018. But he did not have the opportunity as the night before the meeting was to take place, the media announced that he and his staff were dismissed from their jobs. They received US$ three million as compensation, but left with this stain on their curriculums.

The CBF president and his deputy (Marco Polo Del Nero) acted quickly to nominate a new coach. Against the media and street voices who were calling for Tite, they chose Dunga who had served as the Seleção's coach in the 2010 World Cup. Tite who, even before the 2014 World Cup was in the pipeline to be the team's coach, was again left behind by someone who previously had been the team's coach and, just like Felipão, was given another chance.

The CBF's top people nominated Dunga as he was deemed to be a tough guy, with severe discipline, who would put some order in the team after the humiliation at home. Those were the same reasons that were given to Brazilians when Dunga had his first tenure over the national team.

However, unlike Felipão and Tite, Dunga had never been a coach before in his life for any team. His football experience came directly from the field, as a player and captain of the Seleção's 1994 winning team in the US World Cup. Despite being severely criticised for his lack of experience, Dunga took over the team but he was not successful in his first tenure. Even worse, in his second tenure, the team were doing poorly in the South American qualifiers, and was facing the real threat, for the first time in its history, of not qualifying for the World Cup finals. Dunga also engaged in conflict with several players and his relationship with the playing group was visibly worn out.

Marco Polo Del Nero, the man who took over Marin's CBF presidency, was under heavy fire and decided to make the step they should have taken a few years ago. He called Tite to be the *Seleção*'s coach. The same Tite who in 2012, just before winning the FIFA Club World Cup with Corinthians in a game against Chelsea, was the Brazilian people's first choice for the *Seleção*'s top job. He was considered by the majority of the opinion makers as the country's best coach and was finally brought to the seat he should have been sitting in many years beforehand.

The media and the supporters were relieved: the team would stand a chance in the Continental qualifiers. The playing group was also happy, as they would have someone who understood them, and have meaningful conversations, and not lectures about behaviour off the field.

It looked like a miracle, but the *Seleção* was quickly regenerated under Tite's direction. The team not only left sixth position in the South American qualifiers and jumped to first place, but also became the first team besides Russia to have a guaranteed spot in the 2018 World Cup.

Furthermore, the journalists, supporters and the playing group were unanimous in saying that under Tite, the team had recovered the joy of playing football: nobody could believe that in just a few months the *Seleção* would be again playing its best 'futebol-arte' and being once more pointed as one of the favourite teams to win the Russia World Cup.

However, a small detail of this story must be told as well. As the team was winning and playing well, nobody seemed to care about this point, but I consider it to be central to the understanding of the cultural and political dimensions of Brazilian football.

During 2011 and 2012, Tite implemented a contemporary football playing style with the Corinthians. He won the Brazilian Championship and the Copa Libertadores playing amazing football, modern but close enough to what some traditionalists would call 'futebol-arte'.

As I mentioned above, he was rumoured to be the new coach of the *Seleção* for the Brazil World Cup, after the dismissal of Mano Menezes. Marin and Marco Polo did not want him but knew that if he won the FIFA Club World Cup the pressure to appoint Tite would be unsurmountable. So, just before the Club World Cup tournament, they nominated Felipão as the *Seleção's* coach. Tite won the Club World Cup and decided to take a sabbatical in Europe to improve his football knowledge with the world's best clubs. Everybody knows what happened to the team without Tite.

After the 7-1 loss, Tite returned to Brazil and took over Corinthians again. Dunga was appointed, the arrests of FIFA officials happened, and at the end of 2015, the Bom Senso FC and other sporting NGOs organised a manifesto demanding the resignation of the CBF's president, Marco Polo Del Nero and all his board. Dozens of football and politically important names signed off on the manifesto: among them was Tite, who was an important voice calling for "democratic elections for the CBF".

Six months after signing the manifesto, Tite accepted Del Nero's invitation and took over the *Seleção*. After his first press conference as the national team coach, he and the CBF president exchanged a few kisses in stereotypical mafia style.

Tite is an excellent coach and an intelligent man. He knew how symbolic those kisses were. After all, and paraphrasing Ortega y Gasset, a coach is a coach but he is also subject to his coaching circumstances. Even if these circumstances force him to have a Devil's kiss with his enemy of yesterday.

23.

Is the FBI coming?
The nightmares of a Federation president

The Venetian merchant and traveller Marco Polo would not be proud of his Brazilian namesake, Marco Polo Del Nero. During the Brazil World Cup, the Brazilian Del Nero was the deputy-president of the Brazilian Football Federation (CBF) and from April 2015 to December 2017, he occupied the top seat of the sporting body until he was suspended by FIFA due suspicious activities mentioned in the US FIFA trials.

After all, the Venetian is known as one of the greatest explorers in human history; his Asian adventures during the late 13th and early 14th centuries are well-described in the Book of the *Marvels of the World* (aka *The Travels of Marco Polo*) and even still has an impact on readers who are deeply touched by one of the first experiences of the encounters of Western and Eastern civilizations. Marco Polo is a name which will be forever associated with travelling adventures.

The Brazilian Marco Polo cannot travel anymore.

Even as the CBF's President and with all the responsibilities attached to this position, Del Nero did not leave the country to follow the *Seleção* in its numerous competitions away from home. Neither has he attended continental or international football meetings abroad where a Brazilian representative must show up to represent and defend the country's sporting interests. How did this eventuate? Why is this Marco Polo so different to the most famous one whom, as someone of Italian descent, he was surely named after?

Del Nero was not always like that. He used to be a traveller, a first class passenger. As a board member of the CBF and also as the Brazilian representative in FIFA's executive committee, he used not only to travel a lot but also seemed to appreciate his wanders around the world. Brazilians were used to seeing the face of this septuagenarian in the newspapers and on TV, always wearing fine clothes, expensive ties and escorted by young and beautiful girlfriends in luxurious hotels and restaurants during sporting conferences.

After all, he was just taking advantage of his footballing roles' perks of office, and travelling throughout Europe and South America while representing the country for a variety of occasions.

Del Nero's involvement with football management started during the 1980s when he took a few positions within the legal department of Palmeiras Sport Association, the footballing powerhouse which had its origins within the Italian community in São Paulo city. After ascending throughout the club's ranks until being nominated head of the football department, he started to work for one of the most powerful and richest sporting bodies in the country, the São Paulo State Football Federation (FPF). There he climbed the leadership ladder until being elected the FPF's president in 2003.

The FPF chairman's position is a powerful one. Del Nero exerted his power in many ways and not without some turmoil. For example, when he was involved in allegations of refereeing corruption in the final round of the 2008 'Brasileirão' (the National Championship) that saw him receive a 90-day suspension from his position, a punishment that was later reversed by the CBF's courts.

However, he used his influential presidency to become close to the CBF's Ricardo Teixeira. When in 2012 Teixeira had to resign from CBF and from his positions at FIFA to escape further prosecution, Del Nero was appointed as his replacement in the FIFA's executive committee.

Del Nero kept climbing the national footballing power ladder. Was he already seeing the uproar that would implode FIFA a few years later? He has always been a clever man, so he might have seen that, but the power was coming to him and he could not deny it.

In the same year, 2012, Teixeira left the CBF presidency and Marin, as CBF's older vice-president took over the top seat, Del Nero was elected as one of the CBF's regional vice-presidents (Centre-South region). He became close to Marin and, as Marin's tenure would come to an end before the World Cup, they made a deal: Marin would support Del Nero's ambitions to become the CBF's president when the CBF presidential elections were due in the months prior to the World Cup. But Del Nero's term would only start a year later so Marin would enjoy the World Cup as CBF's president.

With Marin's support, Del Nero was elected in April 2014, but remained a deputy till 2015. Then, within just a few weeks of becoming the actual CBF president, he took his last international flight, and then stopped crossing Brazil's borders, and turned into a domestic tourist.

His desire to stay in his country curiously coincided with the 2015 FIFA arrests in Zurich, ahead of the FIFA Congress in May 2015. As CBF's president, Del Nero was there. His close ally and dear friend Marin was present as well. This time, though, Del Nero was much faster than Marin.

As soon as Del Nero heard about the FBI officers arriving at the luxurious Baur au Lac hotel that accommodated FIFA executive committee members, he left everything behind, escaped through a back door, went to the airport and flew straight to Brazil. The small talk is that he was so scared of having the same destiny as Marin, that he did not take any of his belongings or even his escort. He rushed away from Switzerland and did not sleep until he was back in Brazil.

Since then, Del Nero has not left the country. The FBI has no jurisdiction inside Brazil's borders, nor does the United States have an extradition treaty with Brazil, but US authorities could arrest him as soon as he steps outside the country into almost any other country.

The consequences for Brazilian football of not having a powerful voice within South American and international football boards have been awkward: clubs and even the *Seleção* have suffered because of this lack of representation, as discussions and controversial decisions such as competition schedules are always against the Brazilians in their president's absence. Even Rede Globo, the country's major broadcaster which retains the transmission rights of several important competitions such as the Libertadores da America, has been complaining a lot about Del Nero's absences, as this makes it harder to get their preferred TV schedule. Worth mention that the US FIFA trials have also unveiled evidence about the role of Rede Globo in the FIFA briberies scandals.

A small reaction against this situation has been seen in a few blog posts of influential sport journalists such as Juca Kfouri, who always uses a cartoon in his popular online column, saying: 'Fly, Marco Polo, fly'.

Del Nero, though, does not seem to be worried about the comments on his life style. He continued with his everyday life, controlling the CBF with a tight leash for more than two years before being finally suspended by FIFA. He was still seen in luxurious restaurants with his young and beautiful girlfriends. He never talked again with his close friend Marin, who remained in FBI custody in his New York apartment since being arrested in Zurich in 2015, and finally was convicted and incarcerate in December 2017.

His silence speaks a lot. Every CBF local media conference where he was present, the journalists were forbidden to ask if he would attend the next *Seleção*'s match abroad. If someone broke this rule, he simply did not reply and a press attaché interrupted the conference.

His only real worry might be Marin's wife. Neusa Marin, an elegant septuagenarian lady, already disliked Del Nero due to the company that he brought to the dinner table being 'too young,' when both couples were enjoying a CBF- all expenses covered dinner, in fancy restaurants in Europe.

Nowadays she hates him even more for his total lack of support for her husband.

Del Nero did not travel, but the truth did. Marin's testimony in the US FIFA trials provided evidence of Del Nero's involvement in suspicious TV and sponsorship football deals.

After all, the Marins never excused Del Nero for letting Neusa behind and alone in Switzerland in his hurry to escape the FBI. On that day in 2015, the omertà code between these football capos started to break.

24.

The '7-1 syndrome': will Brazilian football never learn?

The *Seleção*'s 7-1 defeat against Germany was one of the lowest points that Brazilian football ever reached in its history. Deemed as a 'new Maracanazo' or even as a "Mineirazo", international commentators were quick to forge stories about potential brawls in Brazilian cities due to that shameful defeat. The international embarrassment of the *Seleção* was completed by the subsequent defeat against Netherlands in the World Cup third place play-off match.

The urban clashes foreseen by some international 'pundits' never occurred. Brazilians are much more mature and their relationship with the team has changed a lot since the 1950 defeat.

As a sign of Brazilian people's greater social consciousness, the 7-1 downfall became a 'negative motto' and started to be used to point out everything about Germany as a society and how it is better than Brazil.

Hence, journalists and people on social media began to compare Germany's educational system structures to Brazil's: outcome? Germany 7-1 Brazil. Germany's economic achievements? 7-1.

The parallels between the countries' social and political landscapes and the consequent use of the '7-1 trashing' allegory was just demonstrating how Brazilians' consciousness is nowadays much more connected to social justice demands than to the *Seleção*'s outcomes.

This is not to say that the *Seleção* does not have any importance for the country's citizens. It still is the symbol and the main sport in Brazil, and Brazilians support and love their team. However, they have grown enough to differentiate what is essential in their lives. The *Seleção* can be a point of relief, national pride and joy among all hardships of everyday life; or can be, as it happened during and after the 2014 World Cup, something to be rejected as a symbol of corrupt practices.

The nasty pathways of the Brazilian team continued after the World Cup, and did not help Brazilians to recover their footballing self-esteem. During Dunga's term, another layer of unhappiness would separate supporters from the team.

With Tite's appointment as head coach, people finally started to feel some footballing joy again. The *Seleção*, which was previously in 6th position in the South American World Cup qualifying tournament, under Tite's command climbed undefeated to the top of the table and became the first national team to have its spot guaranteed in the 2018 World Cup.

Tite, the magician, became an idol. He started to be acclaimed by supporters everywhere he went. Even in the Rio Olympics, when he was just sitting in the stands and enjoying a handball game, the whole stadium started to chant "Ole, ole ole ole – Tite, Tite". The symbiosis between coach, the team and supporters appeared to have returned.

Nevertheless, Tite is transitory. As much as he does for the *Seleção* as its coach, as much as the team plays well and the players are happy. As much as the wins are coming, the people on the streets start to support the team again, and even if the *Seleção* wins the Russia World Cup, Tite is a human being. He has shown his capacity to fight the '7-1 syndrome' on the pitch, making sure that the defeat against Germany stays in world football history as evidence of poor managerial and coaching processes.

However, he cannot change the whole realm of the sport in the country. There is something more in Brazilian football that seems to suffer from a perennial 'off-field 7-1' complex.

Currently, the past CBF's president is imprisoned in New York due to his involvement with the FIFA wrong doings; Teixeira, the once powerful CBF president for more than two decades, faces serious legal troubles due to the same reasons. Furthermore, Marco Polo Del Nero was suspended from his CBF's role by FIFA, and does not travel anymore, fearing the FBI and the FIFA investigations.

Yet, none of these issues have alerted the owners of the game in the country nor the federal authorities, that it is time for a significant reform. Brazilian football needs an in-depth reengineering, not only some cosmetic adjustments, but nobody seems to be able to ignite this more than needed process.

Among several issues, one that urgently needs to be addressed is the national football calendar. Bom Senso FC, journalists and academics have insisted that this is a critical topic but still CBF and Rede Globo hold with an overdue system.

First and second national tier professional clubs usually commence their preseason training by early January. Then, after just two weeks, the State Championships start and go on until the end of April. Major clubs also play the National Championship from April to December, alongside to the Brazilian Cup. Several clubs are also involved in the Libertadores da America (South America Champions League) or the Copa Sul-Americana (the second tier of the Libertadores da America).

All of these competitions are squished in eight months after the State Championships. At the end of the year, a successful top-tier club might have played more than 70 games on that season. This amount of matches is a formula for players' injuries among other disadvantages for the clubs.

Why do these State Championships, which in the last century were relevant and important for regional football development, still occupy nearly a third of the annual football season in Brazil? Why top-tier teams keep playing these tournaments that clearly lost their brilliance when compared to all the other larger and international competitions that Brazilian teams participate in?

The answer is: political power. Football politics.

Despite the economic and sporting supremacy of the Serie A (first national tier) and Serie B (second national tier) clubs in Brazil, and in spite of these clubs collective supporters numbering in their millions around the country, the 27 Football State Federations still detain the power within CBF.

Actually, CBF keeps financial control over those Federations, much of them representing tiny states where professional football practically does not exist. The CBF, by giving monthly grants to these Federations, sustain and dictate the political alliances that write the destiny of football in the country.

As a compensation for their support, the Football State Federations maintain the State Championships at the beginning of the national football calendar for nearly four months. Supported by the CBF, they force the top-tier clubs to play in tournaments with their best players, versing minor teams from small cities. There are teams in the State championships that just open their doors during these initial months of the season as they want to showcase their players to make deals with the big clubs.

The State Championships put top-tier players with multimillion dollar contracts versing underpaid players and minor teams. These tournaments are played in several round-robins for nearly four months. The venues are located in small cities with tiny stadiums. Every club, from the small ones to the Serie A/B clubs is involved during the whole time, before entering in the final knockout phase. The State Federations are the only ones that profit from these old-fashioned competitions. For the clubs though, the advantages of playing there are minimal, either to the minor or to the major ones.

Serie A/B clubs have to commit too much time and resources to play in irrelevant competitions, which do not lead them anywhere. They also risk their best players and do not have decent audiences until the final stages of the tournaments.

On the other hand, the minor clubs, after playing in those competitions, usually do not have anything else to play for the rest of the year, and end up dismissing their teams.

State competitions should exist as pathways for small and medium clubs' expansion and player development. They should be played in a knockout format, with Serie A and Serie B clubs entering there in the final rounds.

The Serie A/B clubs have always tried to organise themselves, creating their parallel competitions and even trying to be independent from the CBF and their most important broadcaster ally, Rede Globo. However, with huge debts to the government and the CBF, the clubs find it difficult to break this vicious cycle.

The clubs also have either no seat or voice in the CBF's board meeting that decides the future of the game in the country. They have no seat where pressing topics such as competition calendars, financing models and all of the most important issues for a football organisation are decided.

In early April 2017, feeling the pressure of the country's most popular clubs, the CBF changed the statutes of its general assembly, and increased the voting power of the state federations. With this modification, each federation's vote equates to 3, in a total of 81 votes. The professional clubs will never have more than 60 votes.

In addition, any person looking to be a candidate for the CBF's top chair must currently have the support of at least eight state federations. The football power circuit in Brazil will remain as closed as possible, with no chance of the more-than-needed alterations to occur in the near future.

Many called these changes in the CBF's general assembly voting as a political master coup to give power to the state federations that represent, according to them, millions of supporters.

More critical perceptions will merely state that this is another '7-1' defeat for Brazilian football.

25.

Who will pay the bill of the best World Cup ever?

Unfinished stadiums; street violence; chaotic traffic; people's unrest; ongoing airport developments; lack of public transport; insufficient internet coverage.

As the World Cup approached, the international media was tracking down every detail of the mega event, and casting shadows on the viability of the football tournament.

As the tournament began and FIFA's powerful media army started to broadcast the matches and the footballing wonders and rivalries, billions of people around the world watched the competition in real time. In Brazil, if you did not call a favela home, living under the National Forces occupation and having your basic human rights violated on a daily basis, or if you had not been evicted from your precarious home to make way for the FIFA circus, and if you had the means to attend the Games, you could be among the crowds, cheering and partying on the stands.

At that stage, Brazilians felt vindicated. Even with the 'Imagine in the World Cup' motto, it was difficult to find anyone who wanted the tournament to be a disaster. After all, it was the country's image and reputation projected on the world stage that was at stake. So, it would be better if they got it right.

Major footballing journalists such as Juca Kfouri, who had been criticizing the CBF's management for the past 20 years and who did not agree with Brazil hosting the tournament, and other influential people were still stating on the eve of the competition that Brazil would fail in delivering stadiums in appropriate conditions for the games. Even they had to step back. The ball was rolling, the competition was under way and the crowds were happy.

Furthermore, the teams' performances were looking good, and the footballing gods were smiling as attacking football was a prime consideration during the World Cup. Matches were delivering goals galore (by the end of the tournament, there were 171 goals in 64 games) including some masterpieces such as Australia's Tim Cahill's volley against Holland or Colombia's James Rodriguez's strike against Uruguay. There were also some nice surprises such as Costa Rica's wins and, of course, the choreographed goal celebrations of Ghana's team.

In addition to the on-field success, there were the parties. Brazilians know how to party!

Official and unofficial festivities were happening in every single corner of the country. The street atmosphere was unbelievable. There were celebrations from Copacabana Beach in Rio to São Paulo's Vila Madalena bohemian neighbourhood, in the hosting cities and in other cities across the country. It did not take long for the pessimist 'Imagine in the World Cup' motto to be replaced by the optimistic 'The best World Cup ever' adage. Happiness and relief were in the air.

An important and unexpected side-effect of the World Cup was the creation of a 'South American brotherhood'. Brazil is the largest country in the subcontinent. The country is a Portuguese-speaking 'island' of 200 million people surrounded by Spanish speaking countries. Brazil has a border with every South American country, but Chile and Ecuador.

During the World Cup, there were not only Argentineans invading their big brother: there were Chileans, Paraguayans, Colombians and other South American communities who wanted to take part in the festivities. The existence of local rivalries and even border tensions in

South America were not an obstacle for anyone who wanted to join in and participate.

Despite all the parties and the celebrations, the World Cup also brought some serious concerns for Brazilian everyday life after the event. If some neighbours were concerned and annoyed with the public celebrations that increased the noise and rubbish levels around public spaces, they were temporary. However, the World Cup Bill which was approved by the Brazilian Parliament and signed off by the then president Dilma Roussef, attracted critics mainly because of the security issues underpinned in that bill.

Progressive sectors in Brazilian society, NGOs and social movements believed that the exaggerated security measures against potential terrorist acts during the event were also an excuse to increase violent prosecution to opposition from State forces. The large amount of anti-terrorism weapons and devices that were bought by the Brazilian Government from Russian companies remained with the host security forces, ready to be used against demonstrators as the World Cup circus left the country. Advanced methods of intimidation against unarmed street demonstrators also showed that the World Cup left a legacy of oppression that will remain in the country long after the tournament finished.

The worries around the World Cup were not only about the infrastructure readiness – they were also linked to the corruption involving billions of taxpayers' money. The historical ties of corruption that have always linked major property developers to all layers of Brazilian government gave many reasons for widespread suspicion about the World Cup works.

As the mega event needed a massive amount of stadiums renovations and new constructions, credit lines were facilitated and the building industry flourished. As the show had to go on, the denunciations of misuse of public funding were lowered in the media; instead, the view was that everything should be covered-up so Brazil could have the best World Cup delivered in a timely manner.

To make things better – for the corrupt, that is -, Rio hosted the Olympics two years later – so more buildings were needed and more public funding was deviated. The accounts of Rio's public employees in not having their wages paid as the state was bankrupt a few months before the Olympics were pungent and raised the question: where did all the invested money for the mega sports events go?

A few years after the event though, the corruption network that used the World Cup and the Olympics as a platform to pour money into politicians' and entrepreneurs' pockets from the public treasury was revealed. Amidst one of the most severe political scandals in the country's history, hundreds of politicians were denounced by their former allies in the business of corruption. The executives and the CEO of one of the largest Brazilian developer company, with Rio de Janeiro's former governor, went to jail. Prominent politicians from nearly all major Brazilian parties were prosecuted for corruption.

These dishonest practices are, unfortunately, common in the country's history and happened before the World Cup. However, the size and scale of the event somehow 'assisted' the corrupted and corrupt to combine in order to illegally profit from public money related to the World Cup works.

The critiques to the event were voiced by people who knew that the central issue for Brazil hosting the event was not the World Cup itself and its associated expenditures, but the large room it would open for corruption around the country. If in Brazil's history, the kinship of politicians, developers and corruption was an integral part of the landscape, can you 'imagine in the World Cup'?

As fantastic as the football parties were during the event, Brazilians are yet to celebrate 'juntos num só ritmo' ("all in one rhythm"®) many years after the 2014 World Cup.

26.

Marta is better than Pelé

No empty seat in the stadiums. The crowd chanting in full voice. The whole country behind the team. It looked like a dream was coming true for the Brazilian female players that were playing for the *Seleção* (yes, the women's team is also known as the *Seleção* – the *Seleção feminina*, or the 'female' *Seleção*) during Rio 2016.

As Neymar's team was not doing well in the first phase of the Olympic tournament, and as Marta's team was flying, playing a nice futebol-arte style and scoring goals, all eyes turned to them. In the past Marta's team had won the Silver Medal at Athens 2004 and Beijing 2012, so this would be the perfect chance for the team to achieve their golden dream.

In the first match of the knockout phase, however, the female *Seleção* nearly missed out. They could not pass through the defensive efforts of the Matildas (the Australian female team) and in the penalty shootout they were nearly eliminated, after the team's captain missed a penalty. But Barbara, the team's goalkeeper, made some amazing saves and put the team on the semi-final route.

Unfortunately, this time the female *Seleção* could not win another penalty shootout against Sweden. Afterwards they went to the Bronze Medal play-off where, without any enthusiasm, they lost to Canada and finished the Rio Olympic tournament in the 4th place.

After this last match, the team's captain pleaded to the whole country: *"please do not stop supporting women's football".*

As she had experienced herself, the captain could envisage that after the Olympic fever was gone the gender status quo within the Brazilian football realm would come back to its routine. Women's football would be left in the margins and everything – from funding to media attention, to clubs support, to audiences – would again be turned towards men's football.

Marta, the team's captain, knew what she was talking about when she made that appeal. She knew that once again she had to take the rare opportunity to talk in front of the entire country to demand their support towards female football.

Marta was conscious that girls and young women still face prejudice and several hurdles when trying to enter Brazilian football fields. From local parks to schools and within the youth system, the barriers are still enormous.

Despite her personal success and amazing international achievements, Marta has suffered her entire life because of her passion for playing a sport that was supposedly not meant to be played by human beings who were born with vaginas. As Brazilians learn before they can even walk – given the gender constructs that have historically surrounded its practice – football is deemed as male terrain.

Marta has jumped many gender obstacles in her footballing journey which, of course, a man would never face. That's why her trajectory is so exceptional. That's why a spectator could raise a banner during the Rio 2007 Pan-American Games stating: "*Who cares about Pelé when you can cheer on Marta!?*".

That's why we can say that Marta is better than Pelé. This is of course a feminist statement but is also supported by Marta's own statistics.

Marta Vieira da Silva has a humble origin. She was born in Alagoas, a poor state in Brazil's northeast. Her rise to the top of women's football was fast. After attracting attention while playing for a local club's (CSA) youth team, she started as a professional at Vasco da Gama, a major club in Rio de Janeiro, when she was only 14 years old.

After a few years, she transferred to play in Sweden for Umeà IK where she started to show her talent to the football world. She played for European and US clubs, and also had some spells with Brazilian clubs in one of the few periods where clubs decided to support women's football.

Marta is the only player in the history of world football – yes, I am talking about any gender here – to have received five times in a row the FIFA award for world's best player (from 2006 to 2010). She is also the greatest goal scorer in the history of the FIFA Women's World Cup with 15 goals so far, followed closely by the German player Birgit Prinz.

Moreover, Marta has surpassed Pelé in goals scored while playing for the *Seleção*. He stopped at 95 goals, Marta has already scored 117 goals wearing the magic yellow jersey, a record that makes her the *Seleção*'s all-times goal scorer. All these stats are solid evidence for my statement that Marta is better than Pelé.

However, there is something else that might place Marta above the 'Football King'. Women's football has always been relegated and even forbidden in Brazil. Hence, for Brazilian girls and women, playing football has always been more than a sporting action: it's a political statement.

As a woman goes into the business of kicking a ball with her feet, she constantly threatens the gender status quo in the most *machista* arena of the country – the football fields.

Marta was never a political or a feminist leader, preferring to demonstrate her political acts within the footballing context. Nevertheless, she has never refused to support the gender agenda that was in front of her. She has always been with her teammates whenever they needed to fight for better conditions for female footballers.

For example, after conquering the Silver Medal in the 2004 Athens Olympics with the female *Seleção*, Marta and the team pressured the infamous Ricardo Teixeira, the CBF president at that time to give more attention to women's football. They sent him a letter, a manifesto emphasising the need for the Federation to appropriately establish women's football in Brazil.

They demanded enough funding and a permanent national team as well as a schedule with regional and national tournaments. In this manifesto, the women clearly stated that no athlete should be chosen based on her body shape, hair, skin colour or image, as happened in the past when the Federation was trying to make football a 'beauty contest' by only selecting young, white and blond players to participate in teams.

If one cannot say that Marta was an activist, she was not someone who was silent either. She has always fought the right battle to advance women's football and hence gender rights in Brazilian society.

Pelé once declared that "Marta is the Pelé who wears skirts".

Future generations may change his statement and simply say that Marta is the best footballer who has ever served the *Seleção*. Full stop.

27.

Cultural and political legacies of the World Cup: where to now? *(with Ramon Spaaij)*

During the 2013 Confederations Cup football tournament in Brazil, hundreds of thousands of demonstrators took to the country's streets to demand change.

Protests that started with a clear opposition to rising public transport fees quickly shifted focus to the enormous amount of government money being spent to host the 2014 World Cup. Demonstrators were waving banners with slogans like:

We don't need the World Cup, we need health and education.

Police used extremely violent measures to stop the protesters, which inflamed the already heated situation.

Similar protests re-appeared during the World Cup. While the world's best football players displayed their talents in brand new stadiums across Brazil and millions of tourists were enjoying the 'best World Cup ever', they also witnessed political protests and occasionally mixed with demonstrators.

Sporting mega-events like the World Cup are always accompanied by lofty promises on their lasting legacy for the host country. In Brazil and elsewhere, such legacy planning helps justify the billions spent on Organising and hosting the event. So what kind of legacy has the World Cup left in Brazil?

Economic versus cultural and political legacy

The legacy of sporting mega-events is often perceived in economic terms, with a focus on benefits to employment, tourism, infrastructure and urban renewal. During the World Cup, numbers are clearly an important part of legacy analysis, but they are far from being the only contributing factor to the overall legacy. It is at the sociocultural and political levels that the legacy of the World Cup may be felt the most.

Sporting mega-events do not happen in a social vacuum. They have to account for the past, the present and even the future of the communities involved. The World Cup is hosted by countries with remarkable histories where social changes are constantly occurring, sometimes at a rapid pace.

2014 was an important year for Brazil. It had been 60 years since Getulio Vargas – one of the most remarkable elected presidents in Brazilian history – committed suicide. 2014 also marked the 50th anniversary of the coup d'état that installed the 21-year military dictatorship: another historic milestone that continues to bring bad memories for Brazilians.

In 2014, Brazilians also celebrated the 30th birthday of the Diretas Já! (Free Elections Now) movement, which mobilised millions of protesters to take to the streets for the first time since the 1964 military coup. Despite its ultimate goal of direct elections being initially defeated by the Brazilian Parliament, this movement opened the door for the re-democratization of Brazil after 21 years of dictatorial rule.

Finally, a few months after the World Cup, Brazilian citizens elected their federal government in what was the seventh straight democratic presidential election – a record in the country's history.

Infrastructure changes

The legacy of any World Cup is highly contentious. The event temporarily increases the number of tourists and jobs. In Brazil, it has also brought quality football stadiums to a country where these have long been in a bad state.

At the same time, the World Cup put the alleged corruption surrounding stadium construction under global scrutiny. In a clear waste of public money, some of the new facilities became white elephants after the World Cup as there would be no spectators to fill them. Forced relocations in the past few years profoundly affected several disadvantaged communities in the years before the event.

Upgrades to airports and public transport have taken place. However, this has been a slow process. Some upgrades were not completed in time for the tournament. The promised urban mobility legacy is still to come to fruition e v e n after the tournament had ended.

An unanticipated legacy

One of the most notable legacies of the World Cup may yet be its unanticipated political legacy. Even before its opening, the event had magnified and given a global platform to the social movements that had been on Brazilian society's margins in the last decade; it accelerated the democratic battle that is still underway in Brazil.

On one side, progressive movements pushed for an expansion of the social agenda. On the other, conservative powers seek to erase the recent social improvements through the use of both their mass media power and state repression.

In addition, Brazilians now want to know the truth about their recent history.

The government and civil society have at last started to open the secret files that show the army's involvement in systematic torture and killing of the opposition during the military's ruling.

Anti-democratic forces that supported the dictatorship are still present within the army and the police. They continue to use torture, illegal detention and physical elimination to silence their opponents, and they infiltrate social movements in order to create chaos in any peaceful civil demonstration.

Meanwhile, other political legacies emerged during the tournament. The federal government reportedly spent nearly U$670 million on policing the World Cup in a bid to suppress potential disturbances.

In a period when Brazil is still searching for the truth about the dictatorship period, the heavy hand imposed on demonstrators and anti-World Cup activists was a clear undemocratic throwback. The new repression strategies left a political scar of profound disregard for human rights, which Brazilians will have to overcome in order to build their immature democracy.

The concern over forced relocations also cannot be forgotten. The vulnerable people who were removed from their houses have the right not only to receive a new house, but also to be consulted on where they want to live. These places must have sufficient social support to enable the displaced people to quickly readjust to their new lives.

So far, this is the major negative legacy of the World Cup, one that has to be remembered every day until the right solutions are found.

Football legacy

Finally, the impact the World Cup already made on Brazil's football culture cannot be underestimated. There were a few white elephant stadiums, such as Cuiaba's Arena Pantanal, that were specifically built for the World Cup and was unable to attract enough supporters to sustain it. Cuiaba's regional football tournament has an average attendance of less than 1,000.

The shocking semi-final defeat against Germany (1-7) certainly left a perennial blot on Brazil's football culture and history. The failures in the Seleção's preparation and in the entire structure of the Brazilian

Football Federation were not enough scrutinised. Change is crucial if Brazil wants to keep its historical dominance over the international football world, which was seriously under threat after many years of a lack of direction for the *Seleção*.

Brazilian football, as a central element of the country's culture, needs urgent political and cultural revolution. But will this revolution be one of the most important political and cultural legacies of the 'best World Cup ever'?

28.

Brazil 3014: A Garrincha-Sócrates dream or a Havelange-Teixeira nightmare?

Conceive that in the early stages of the 22nd century, Brazilian authorities are again considering a bid for the 3014 World Cup. As it has been nearly 100 years since Brazil hosted its last World Cup, it is time to celebrate this centenary, they argue. Thereby, in a fictional exercise, let's think through this bidding process to see whether it would be a good idea for the country to ever host this event again. Of course, this exercise depends on whether the whole world will survive until the next century, as at the moment humanity faces many challenges that look unsurmountable, such as global warming and the prospect of a worldwide nuclear war.

By looking at the 2014 event through historical accounts, they show from the onset that just the idea of hosting the mega football event in 2014 was severely criticised in that period. Given the social inequalities that were abounding throughout the country a hundred years earlier, it actually did not look like a great idea to spend public money on football stadiums.

This was the general impression of many people not only in Brazil but also around the world. These voices claimed that educational and health systems should be prioritised when public money expenditure was at stake.

On the other hand, Brazil's bid to host the event received strong support from federal, state and local governments. From the usual arguments that the event would boost international tourism to the country, thus generating jobs and bringing money to the national economy; to the most political aspects of promoting the country's image to the world;

and also, from developers and politicians that saw the event as a chance to augment their profits, the World Cup bid was well backed and successful.

Another rationale that emerged in the past and which looked more balanced was the argument that, indeed, hosting the World Cup would be beneficial for the country in many aspects. It would advance more than needed infrastructure building such as subways and airports. In footballing terms, this rationale also could foresee that new and modern stadiums would be advantageous for sport performances, both for players and for supporters.

However, this rationale was emphatic that a World Cup should not be organised by the same people that had always controlled football in the country. In summary, if hosting the World Cup undeniably could be a great thing for Brazil, with the actual people who would work to put the event together (CBF and FIFA officials, Rede Globo, politicians and their friends in the development industry to name a few), the chances for more corruption and misuse of tax payer's scarce money were high.

In 3014, though, these assessments became clearer. The historical perspective demonstrated that the 2014 World Cup combined several aspects.

It was a dream coming true for real Brazilian football lovers. For a few weeks, the spirits of Sócrates and Garrincha were alive once again in the country. Football-art was being played in excellent venues while people partied on the streets. Political consciousness raised and demonstrators demanded better public services while marching against corrupt authorities.

Educational projects based on the World Cup were bringing authentic learning experiences for students. Gender activists promoted live activities to raise the importance of footballing opportunities for girls and women in the country.

On the other hand, the footballing nightmares continued to haunt Brazilian people. Havelange's ghosts in the form of CBF and World Cup organising committee authorities were connected to the military dictatorship and also to the 'money laundry' that took advantage of the event to subtract millions of public funding to their bank accounts.

Political prosecution and tough repression against social activists were an increasing reality before, during and after the tournament. Economic elites took advantage of their proximity to the country's president to humiliate her, showing their misogynistic faces. Furthermore, a confusing sporting plan left its scars on Brazilian football history and after many years people were still talking about the *Seleção* being smashed in their home semi-final against Germany.

Hence, with all these conflicting legacies, would Brazil be ready and willing to host another World Cup in 3014?

Anticipating the challenges that the country might face when this proposal comes through, I propose an agenda that needs to be executed before Brazil raises its hand to host the event again.

These are not simple topics but must be done in order for the country achieve its profound democratic and cultural potential.

1. Football, together with other sports, needs to be put in the centre of an agenda that encourages social health across the country. Football should be considered bigger than a competition played by 22 people, but it needs to be acknowledged as a cultural factor of community development, hence planned and funded for these objectives.

2. Gender equality in football must be a reality: boys and girls need to have the same opportunities to play and enjoy the game everywhere, from school yards to professional fields.

3. CBF and all state federations need to be dismantled and their managers prosecuted and thrown into jail when found guilty after a fair trial. The money they deviated recovered. Community bodies are to be built to replace these former sporting bodies; their boards are to be elected every three years according to their performances; their activities are to be totally transparent for the communities involved.

4. The crimes perpetrated by the military dictatorship have finally been resolved. Families recovered the bodies of their relatives who disappeared during the 1964-1985 dictatorship; all archives came to light and the culprits received a fair trial and went to jail; all football spaces that were named after people connected to the dictatorship were renamed to celebrate local community leaders;

5. Indigenous people have their rights acknowledged, their cultural traditions respected and their lands demarked;

6. Brazilians have finally realised that the change that they need will not come from authorities in Brasilia, but from their well-organised communities. Schools in the country became key spaces for social transformation and football is an important part of this process;

7. Havelange-Teixeira ghosts had finally been expelled from the country; the only spirits that reign are from a range of Martas, Sócrates and Garrinchas that happily play on Brazilian fields, from the North to the South.

Lastly, Brazilians realised that they do not need a mega sport event to show off the country's prowess's. The 3014 World Cup, then, is based in the social justice achievements of the country. It promises an event based on local communities, where everyone will have the right to access the benefits brought by a clean and sustainable event, where the *Seleção* will shine but also contribute to the development of the broader society.

They are yet to charge for our dreams.

AFTERWORD
by Luiz Guilherme Piva

Amongst his many qualities, Jorge Knijnik shows a very special one: he is able to watch and see the world much better than us. One need just to read a few chapters of his book to realize that Jorge not only sees what we cannot see, despite being clearly exposed in front of us; he can also unveil and enlighten what is hidden from all of us.

This is exactly what he does with the 2014 Brazil World Cup. Where we just see a football tournament, he also perceives a country, its people, its history, its cultural diversity, its issues and its possible futures. Where we only see football matches he identifies economic, social and political structures.

Additionally, Jorge sees the 'others', the ones who were not in the World Cup, who were excluded from the party; furthermore, the ones who were harmed by the mega event. Hence, his chapters when talking about the football field, line up also topics such as gender, education, poverty, violence, exclusion and everything else that, in contrast with the World Cup's glow, was pushed to the shadows in front of our eyes.

Jorge brings to the surface the very truth we either pretend not seeing or we are not able to perceive: the real Brazil's World Cup played by Brazilian people is much lengthier than the one-month tournament. It runs across our history in the past centuries and there is still plenty to be played in the future years. Jorge sets wide open the basic and tough facts: in this game Brazil is losing for a much larger score than the 7x1 against Germany, who smashed Brazil in the World Cup semi-final.

Maybe Jorge's exterior perspective helps him to have a better look at what is actually happening to his country. Perhaps the large ocean that separates him in Australia from us in Brazil allow him to dive into our profound secrets and to look at our more invisible dimensions.

Most importantly, though, is that, in both hypotheses, he shows his deep knowledge about what he writes and his love for his work. We have to commend his talent and the pleasure he analyses football and everything that permeates this sport in Brazil.

After reading this book, someone would say that football is part of the Brazilian 'culture', in the anthropological meaning. I do not like this conceptual framework, as it refers to national identities and singularities, which are analytical categories that have always been mistaken and are much more nowadays, when even the global physical frontiers have been dismantled. Moreover, I don't think this is Jorge's main idea.

As I read through all chapters of this excellent book, my views over Brazil and football have been reinforced: football has never defined Brazil's arguably single identity and culture; instead, as regarded and described by Jorge Knijnik, it is Brazil as a country, with its diversity, its difficulties, its qualities and its challenges that gives to football its uniqueness as a sport. Brazil is football's own particular country.

Thank you, Jorge, for guiding us with your sharp eyes.

Luiz Guilherme Piva is a Brazilian economist and political scientist who also writes on football. He has authored Eram todos camisa dez ('They were all number 10'), published by Iluminuras, amongst other books.

BIBLIOGRAPHY

Alvito, Marcos 'Our Piece of the Pie: Brazilian Football and Globalization', *Soccer & Society*, vol. 8, no. 4, 2007, pp. 524-44.

Bellos, Alex Futebol: *the Brazilian Way of Life*, Bloomsbury, London, 2002.

Curi, Martin (ed). *Soccer in Brazil*, Routledge, New York, 2015.

Downie, Andrew. *Doctor Sócrates: footballer, philosopher, legend.* London, Simon & Schuster, 2017.

Duarte, Fernando. *Shocking Brazil*: Six days that shook the World Cup, Edingburgh, Birliinn Ltd, 2014.

Florenzano, Jose, A *Democracia Corinthiana: Práticas de Liberdade no Futebol Brasileiro* [Corinthians Democracy: Freedom Practices in Brazilian Football], Educ/Fapesp, São Paulo, 2010.

Fontes, Paulo (ed.) and Hollanda, Bernardo Borges Buarque de (ed.). The country of football: politics, popular culture & the beautiful game in Brazil. Londres: Hurst & Co, 2014.

Franco Junior, A *Dança dos Deuses: Futebol, Sociedade, Cultura* [The Gods dance: football, society, culture], Companhia das Letras, São Paulo, 2007.

"Gente grande," *Folha de São Paulo*, 3 Oct. 2009.

Gordon, Cesar and Ronaldo Helal, 'The Crisis of Brazilian Football: Perspective for the Twenty-first Century', *International Journal of the History of Sport*, vol. 18, no. 3, 2001, pp. 139-58

Helal, Ronaldo and Antonio Jorge Soares, 'The Decline of the 'Soccer-Nation': Journalism, Soccer and National Identity in the 2002 World Cup', *Soccer & Society*, vol. 15, no. 1, 2014, pp. 132-46.

Hollanda, Bernardo Borges Buarque de. In Praise of Improvisation in Brazilian Soccer: Modernism, Popular Music, and a Brasilidade of Sports. *Critical Studies in Improvisation/Études critiques en improvisation* 2011; 7(1).

Kittleson, Roger, The Country of Football: *Soccer and the Making of Modern Brazil*, University of California Press, Berkeley and Los Angeles, 2014

Knijnik, Jorge, 'Visions of Gender Justice: Untested Feasibility on the Football Fields of Brazil', *Journal of Sport and Social Issues*, vol. 37, no. 1, 2013, pp. 8-30

Knijnik, Jorge, 'Playing for Freedom: Sócrates, Futebol-arte and Democratic Struggle in Brazil', *Soccer & Society*, vol. 15, no. 1, 2014, pp. 635-54

Lirio S. (editor) *Sócrates Brasileiro: as crônicas do Doutor em Carta Capital.* São Paulo: Editora Confiança, 2012. [Sócrates Brasileiro: Doctor's chronicles in Carta Capital].

Natali, M. The Realm of the Possible: Remembering Brazilian Futebol. *Soccer & Society* 2007;8 (2/3):267-82.

Pardue D. Jogada Linguistica: Discursive Play and the Hegemonic Force of Soccer in Brazil. *Journal of Sport & Social Issues* 2002; 26(4):360-80.

Piva, Luiz Guilherme. Eram todos camisa Dez [They were all number 10]. São Paulo, Iluminuras, 2013.

Raspaud, Michel *Histoire du Football au Bresil*, Chandeigne, Paris, 2010.

Ribeiro Jr , Amaury; Leandro Cipoloni; Luiz Carlos Azenha and Tony Chastinet, *O Lado Sujo do Futebol: A Trama de Propinas, Negociatas e*

Traições que Abalou o Esporte Mais Popular do Mundo [The Dirty Side of Football: The Plot of Briberies, Horse-tradings and Betrayals that Convulsed the World's Most Popular Sport], Editora Planeta do Brasil, São Paulo, 2014.

Rolnik, Raquel et al. (eds). *O Brasil em Jogo: o que Fica da Copa e das Olimpíadas?* [Brasil at Play: What Will Be the Legacy of the World Cup and the Olympics?] Carta Maior, São Paulo, 2014.

Santos Neto, José Moraes dos, *Visão do Jogo: Primórdios do Futebol no Brasil* [Understanding the Game: Earliest Days of Football in Brazil], Cosac & Natify, Rio de Janeiro, 2002.

Saldanha, João. Os *subterrâneos do futebol* (Rio de Janeiro: Tempo Brasileiro, 1963), 214.

Sócrates and R. Gozzi. *Democracia Corintiana: a utopia em jogo.* São Paulo: Boitempo, 2002. [Corinthians Democracy: the utopy in question].

Toledo, L. H. No país do futebol. 1. ed. Rio de Janeiro: Zahar Editor, 2000.

Wisnik, JM. *Veneno remédio: o futebol e o Brasil: Companhia das Letras* São Paulo, 2008

Zirin, Dave. *Brazil's Dance with the Devil: The World Cup, The Olympics, and the struggle for Democracy.* Chicago: Haymarket Books, 2014.

ACKNOWLEDGEMENTS

I would like to acknowledge Piva, Roger, Mildred, Miriam and Ramon for their terrific contributions to this book; Paul for his valuable work as language editor of my chronicles; Bonita Mersiades and the Fair Play Publishing crew for believing in my writings. Peter Horton, Bob Petersen, Bill Murray and Chris Hallinan for being the most supportive friends ever.

I would like also to recognise great grassroots footballers who keep the game alive: MaguiLeo, Cleiton, Suzana, Clio, Alan (BRFC), Osmar, Tó, Xivone, Miguel e Marcelinho.

Most of all, I would like to send all my love to my family in Brazil and in Australia, who always support my writing endeavours: my beloved father **Carlos**, who introduced me to the World Game during unforgettable evenings at the Pacaembu Stadium; my adored mother **Olga** who constantly fed my football team after countless hours of street games; my much-loved wife **Selma**, who tolerates my loud voice in front of the TV screen; my treasured daughters Lulu, the best friend on the stands; **Marinoca**, who knows how to cheer; **Juju**, my favourite writer; and my precious son **Alezão**, who will forever be the smiling player!

Jorge Knijnik

Want some more really good football books from Fair Play Publishing?

Encyclopedia of Socceroos - Every National Team Player
by Andrew Howe

Coming Soon:

Australia, Asia and the First Socceroos
by Trevor Thompson

Courage Under Fire - the Goalkeeper's Bible
by Jim Fraser

Support Your Local League
by Antony Sutton

From our US partners, Powderhouse Press of Wyoming:

Whatever It Takes - the Inside Story of the FIFA Way
by Bonita Mersiades

www.fairplaypublishing.com.au

CPSIA information can be obtained
at www.ICGtesting.com
Printed in the USA
LVHW070445081221
705584LV00005B/57